SILVER THREADS

SILVER THREADS

A LIFE ALONE

John Williams

BBC BOOKS

Published by BBC Books,
a division of BBC Enterprises Limited,
Woodlands, 80 Wood Lane, London W12 0TT

First Published 1994

ISBN 0 563 36941 8

Set in 10½pt Linotron Trump by
Phoenix Photosetting, Chatham, Kent
Printed and bound in Great Britain by
Butler & Tanner Ltd, Frome and London
Jacket printed by
Lawrence Allen Ltd, Weston-super-Mare

Acknowledgements
My thanks go to Doug Young for editing the manuscript while keeping to its spirit. Thanks also to Heather Holden-Brown, Senior Commissioning Editor at BBC Books, for believing that *Silver Threads* should be published.

Since coming out of prison I've received much love and support from the following people. My thanks to Dinah John Liberty and Asa Beryl Roden, Dave Spanswick, Helena Uren, John Yeoman, Howard Coster – who unfortunately is back in prison – and the regulars of the Martha Gunn pub, particularly Kevin who often slipped me a fiver when he suspected I was broke.

CHAPTER 1

IN THE WINTER OF 1948 I COMMITTED THE OFFENCE OF BEING born. Three months later, I was handed into the care of Dr Barnardo's Village Homes at Barkingside in Essex. About the time of the Queen's Coronation in 1953, a new Matron took over from the previous house parents. All the cottages in the Village were flying flags of red white and blue, and the Village green was covered with brightly painted stalls. The main gates, fixed between the surrounding brick walls, were open wide with outsiders and insiders forming one big happy crowd. Matron had sent me out from the cottage with a bright silver sixpence. Each child in the cottage had been given one to spend and I had kept mine clutched tightly in my hand all afternoon.

When the Punch and Judy show began, I watched as if spellbound. I'd never seen anything like this – Mr Punch screaming at Judy, Judy screeching back, loud whacks from the stick as it beat on Judy's head. Then the baby got killed and a policeman arrived to look for Mr Punch.

'Where's Mr Punch?' he called out.

'Over there!' we all shouted back.

The policeman led Punch away and the show was over. A man moved amongst the audience with a bag into which people were dropping money but I walked away before he got near. I wanted to keep my sixpence. It was far too precious to spend, even on candyfloss. I saw two ladies covered in black with large silver crosses on chains around their necks. One of them was shaking a tin and, just like at the Punch and Judy show, people were giving money. Without thinking I went over and dropped my sixpence through the slot. Suddenly I knew what it was like to feel good as both nuns knelt on the grass, hugged me and said, 'God bless you.'

The other children living in the cottage were between the ages of three and nine. It's difficult to remember individuals because some would leave and others took their place and after a while I only noticed Matron who I imagined would always be there, in charge. On her days off, Matron was replaced by Miss Phillips who wore a deaf aid and seemed ancient. Once I organized the other children to get out of their beds in the middle of the night so that we could go downstairs and give the cottage a surprise spring clean. Miss Phillips appeared in her nightdress and told us all to get undressed and, while we stood there naked, told us off and explained that she had been scared out of her wits imagining there were burglars in the cottage.

My education began at the Village primary school but I was soon transferred. Gearies was about a mile from the Village and I was sent there because apparently my reading ability was advanced for my age. This meant getting used to two names. There was another John Williams in the Village and after my disappointment – and tears – when I was invited to a birthday party by mistake Matron had changed my name to Tony. At Gearies I was still John.

Being big enough to go to an outside school also meant getting used to peeling potatoes. Before leaving in the morning I had to fill a pot with them and make sure no black bits could be found on inspection. Most days,

Matron would be nearby washing the sheets I'd soaked the night before. Wetting the bed was in part a response to terror. One night I woke to see a giant grey figure with piercing green eyes looking down at me. I was sure it was there to kill me. 'Come on, hurry up!' it said. 'Get off that pot – there's others waiting to use it.' Every night I expected the ghost to return and I'd wake with my heart pounding so loud that the sound became footsteps climbing up the stairs to get me. I couldn't move, nor had I the courage to scream. All I could do was pray in desperation to Father God that if only He would make the morning come quickly, or if only Matron would come, I would promise to be good for ever.

It was then that I began to believe them when they called me 'thief'. I began to feel that Matron was watching to see what I stole next. At night she would search my pyjamas and the bed where I slept. It didn't matter to me what the objects I would sneak into bed were: clothes pegs or safety pins would do but it never occurred to me to tell Matron that I was afraid of being alone in the dark. I was only seven, but was already beginning to accept the idea that, if nothing else, one thing was certain: I *was* a thief.

The half-crown dinner-money given to me on Monday mornings was my first step into more lucrative thieving. I spent it in a sweet shop near school. A gang of kids from the playground came with me because I convinced them that they could choose whatever they wanted. I knew that Matron would soon discover what I'd done but I was learning that there were places in my mind where I could hide from future events I didn't want to deal with. There were at least six other kids in the sweet shop that day, so how could I get all the blame? This self-delusion seemed to have come true when Matron said very little about the affair. The following Monday though, she began to use a more secure method of paying for my meals. But there were other places to steal from, like school desks and coats hanging on pegs in empty cloakrooms.

One midmorning break time I heard my name being called from the street side of the playground railings. It was the mother of a boy in my class. She smiled, asked if I came from the Village, then passed a paper bag through the gap in the bars with a sandwich, an apple and some chocolate inside. I was thrilled. It didn't matter that she also asked me to stop stealing her son's packed lunch from the pocket of his mackintosh in the cloakroom.

Walking to school and back home to the cottage meant passing near to the Village hospital, the one building I didn't even dare to glance at. I had spent some time there as a baby, but didn't remember that. Once I had cut a deep gash in my finger with a knife I was helping to dry with a tea towel. Matron was seriously unnerved by the amount of blood and took me to the casualty department of the hospital, which didn't seem such a terrible place after all. The doctor patched me up with a couple of stitches and any residual fear of the hospital was swept away by the bag of sweets I was given for being so brave.

On my way to school the next day I made a slight detour and revisited the casualty department. I didn't expect more sweets but I reckoned if I told a story about being sent by Matron with a sore throat I might get a packet of lozenges. I wanted to be like the other children at school who arrived with treats. Of course I should have known not to push too far. The story worked and lozenges were dispensed, but I thought this meant I could return on a regular basis. A couple of weeks later, the doctor who had stitched my finger decided I needed a week in the isolation ward of the hospital so he could keep an eye on my troublesome throat complaint. Instead of school that day I was dressed in a hospital gown and put to bed in a small cubicle separated from similar rooms by ceiling-to-floor plate-glass windows.

It was no fun being in hospital. The only distraction was the picture puzzles offered by the nurse and I'd always found them really boring. In the afternoon of my third day I was starting to feel seriously sorry for myself. To make matters worse, the boy in the cubicle next to me was having great fun as he bounced up and down on his bed. I began to find his movements quite hypnotic. Images of Coronation Day and the thrill of puppets flying in the air came rushing back. A strange warm feeling made my body tremble. I felt a pleasure I'd never known before as his pyjama jacket flapped open to give me tantalizing glimpses of his small red nipples and golden skin. I left the hospital with a hunger which has persisted to this day. Soon after getting back to school, nervous and excited, I began enticing boys into the toilet and getting them to lift up their vest or open the buttons on their shirt.

It was Matron who told me the news. I was to see the Village psychiatrist, Dr Edwards. On Fridays I was to come home to the cottage for lunch so as to be in good time for the regular afternoon appointment. I was impressed. I felt I'd gained some special status. Not many other kids in the Village had their own doctor to talk to as well as the privilege of being allowed home from school early to see him.

He invited me to sit in the only comfortable chair in his office and we talked about grown-up things like how a man and woman made babies. I enjoyed being with the Doctor but I wouldn't let him put me to sleep. Every week he would try, suggesting I closed my eyes and listen to him tell me how tired I was feeling. I didn't much like the way his voice changed. There was a tone which put me on my guard, something I didn't trust. The best part of the visits was saying goodbye when the doctor played the regular game of tossing sweets in the air and juggling. I had to

5

guess in which hand he concealed them and it wasn't often he was able to fool me.

By the time I was eight I intuitively knew I was missing out on many of the privileges of childhood. Matron thought I should join an outsiders' cub pack but that didn't last long once she learnt I spent most of these Tuesday evenings wandering the streets.

It seemed easier not to turn up and spend my unpaid subs on more sweets. On one of these evenings I walked into the police station which stood just outside the Village walls. I wanted to ask a policeman if he would show me the place where bad men where kept. A uniformed constable said he would and, using a big silver key, unlocked a heavy oak door. To my immense disappointment, the cell was empty. I had hoped to see a lot more.

There were also other, official evenings spent away from the Village which Matron approved. On Wednesdays and Saturdays, I visited Aunt Sylvia's house, the mother of a boy in my class. I first met her waiting outside the school gates to take Stephen, her son, home on the bus. I had always found it easy talking to strangers and when they learned that I lived in the Village there would often be the chance of a gift. Mrs Hastings was no exception and soon arranged with Matron for me to visit.

The first occasion was a complete revelation. The house in Knight's Way immediately felt so different to the cottage where I lived. It was alive. Even the household objects seemed to breathe. I sat in the lounge watching Rin Tin Tin on the television. I knew I was going to be given some tea but was amazed at how relaxed Aunty was about eating from the plates on our laps. We had always had to sit up straight at the table and we never started a meal before saying Grace. Aunty Sylvia must have had more than just a passing sympathy that I didn't have a family of my own. She gave me my first real birthday party at her house. At

Christmas and on other occasions she always gave me presents. Even when I stole from her son's room her kindness didn't falter. I was quite aware that Stephen disliked me and would have preferred me not to visit but I didn't care.

Much to my surprise, Matron would often confront me with evidence of my latest theft almost as soon as I'd done it. The worst she would ever do was send me to bed early or threaten to send me to Colonel Atkins, the Village superintendent, for the cane. One afternoon, however, was very different. She just blurted out the words as I was finishing my tea. 'Tomorrow you'll be moving into a new cottage on the temporary side of the Village.' At first this didn't sink in: Matron had always been in charge and I could never leave her and the cottage. How could she say such a thing?

I sat for a moment, unable to breathe, then felt something break inside me. I began retching painfully and each spasm produced more tears. I never saw Matron again.

CHAPTER 2

THE NEW COTTAGE ON THE OTHER SIDE OF THE VILLAGE WAS
run by Miss Thompson. I wasn't Tony any more, but John
again. There was other advantages: there was a television
and Miss Thompson wasn't as strict as Matron. I'd been in
the new place for a few weeks when Miss Thompson asked
me if I would like to have a new Aunty and Uncle. I said I
would, but I wasn't particularly excited when she told me
that a lady and gentleman would be coming to visit me on
the following Sunday afternoon. I assumed they would be
like the Aunties and Uncles I'd had before, who had turned
up at the cottage, taken me on a day trip to somewhere like
Southend and then had never returned. One Christmas, I'd
been taken to be a companion for a little boy with red hair
who, his mother told me, suffered from nightmares. I
made the mistake of saying I didn't like the boy and had
been promptly returned to Matron. Anyway I still had
Aunty Sylvia's house to visit every Wednesday and Saturday and that was enough for me.

I was quite impressed when my visitors arrived. They
spoke with posh accents and I imagined they must be very
rich, which meant I might be in for all sorts of presents.
The lady was tall and thin. The man had a shiny bald patch
on the top of his head.

8

Miss Thompson suggested I show the couple round the Village. As we walked, I learned that he worked for an insurance company, and his wife was a teacher at a young ladies' secretarial college. I naturally assumed that they were the owners of both concerns. Towards the end of the tour round the Village they asked if I would like to call them Aunty Sylvie and Uncle Horace. I said that would be alright, but I thought it very strange because I already had an Aunty Sylvia and (although I didn't see him very often because he worked away from home a lot) I knew Aunty Sylvia's husband was Uncle Horace.

After they had left the Village, Miss Thompson explained to me that there was a chance that I might be able to go and live with my afternoon visitors for good. She told me that the couple were looking for a child of about eight who needed a new mother and father. Then the pieces came together and I realized why I was now living in the temporary part of the Village. Before then I hadn't realized what the word meant. I remembered a conversation I'd had with a lady I'd never seen before when I was living at the cottage with Matron. That day, Matron had seemed strangely cross and had sent me to the administration offices for some trifling offence she would normally have brushed aside. I thought she had finally decided to carry out her threat to send me to the Colonel for the cane. She told me to report to Miss Toates who I knew well from the Village. She had often visited the cottage and had once given me a bag of toffees because I had nearly stopped biting my nails for a week.

Miss Toates was smiling when I walked into her office and seemed unconcerned when I explained why Matron had sent me. She was more interested in me talking to another lady in the room, the lady I had never seen before. Miss Toates said she had to go to a meeting and the lady began to ask me all kinds of questions: Was I happy at school? What about the Village? Did I have lots of friends? After more questions she suggested we go out into the sunshine.

We stopped near the slide and the swing where she asked me, if I had a mum and dad, what sort of people would I like them to be? I said that they would have to be kind. I wouldn't want them to have any other children and we would live on a farm with a dog and a horse. (I had wanted to include a monkey but I thought I'd better not.) I had never seen the lady since and had soon forgotten the conversation.

On the Friday I was due to spend my first full weekend with my new Aunty and Uncle I ran to school as fast as my legs would carry me. I was convinced that the sooner I got there the more swiftly the day would pass. I couldn't have been more excited. In my tummy there was a warm bubbling feeling. Soon, I kept telling myself, I'll be away from the Village for two whole days and living in a normal outsiders' house. Once the final bell rang, I raced through the school gates like a hare back to the Village. I didn't even bother to stop at the greengrocers to be given my daily apple.

My new Uncle was already there at the cottage waiting for me. Outside the door stood his shiny black Austin Cambridge. Cars were an unusual sight inside the Village and driving slowly towards the main gates I saw faces turning curiously to see who was in such a grand vehicle. I felt so proud, so special. I wanted everybody in the world to see me sitting up high on the front seat next to Uncle. He said that we were going to a place called Staines. I'd never heard of the place but I didn't care. I would have gone anywhere.

That weekend, the only similarity with life in the Village was on Sunday morning. I still had to go to church. Aunty took me to the door, gave me sixpence to put in the collection plate and warned me to be careful crossing the road on the way home. It wasn't church that I minded so much as the reminder that it was Sunday and almost time for me to return to the Village. I didn't want to go back to a place where everyone wore the same clothes and ate the same type of food off the same sort of plastic plate. I didn't want to see another bathroom with labelled toothbrushes laid out in military lines, each one carrying the regulation amount of toothpaste. I wanted to stay with Aunty and Uncle where there were new things to live with, different cups to drink from and carpets on the floor.

As Uncle drove back through the Village gates I bent my head below the dashboard as if to tie my shoe lace. I was ashamed and preferred nobody to see that I had come back. Aunty and Uncle said goodbye at the door of the cottage, promising to return for me on the following Friday. I think Aunty was about to kiss me but I ran into the cottage before she could.

I spent every weekend for six months away from the Village getting used to life with Aunty and Uncle in Staines. I was to move in with them permanently at the end of the summer term. With so many weekends away from the Village I was beginning to feel like a stranger there. In fact, ever since leaving Matron I'd felt as if I no longer belonged.

On the last day of term I sat cross-legged on the floor of the assembly hall and waited for my name to be called out by the head teacher. A couple of weeks earlier I had taken part in the annual sports day and had won seven events which meant I would be eligible for one of the overall winner's medals. There was a rule that a maximum of six events could be entered, so I wasn't sure whether I'd disqualified myself from a prize. My name was eventually called out and I walked up onto the stage with the applause of the entire school ringing round the hall. At any moment

I expected someone to shout out that I'd taken part in too many events but nothing was said. The head teacher congratulated me, shook me by the hand and presented me with a red velvet-lined box in which lay a silver medal. Walking back to my place amongst my classmates the thought struck me soon I would be gone with the medal safe in my hands. Then the whole school sang the hymn, 'God be with you till we meet again'. I found it hard to hold back the tears. I didn't want to say goodbye to the teachers and my friends. Leaving the Village was much easier though. It was just like I was going away for the weekend again, but this time I knew it was for good.

CHAPTER 3

EVERYTHING SEEMED TO BE GOING WELL IN MY NEW HOME until I started asking questions about the lady in my bedroom. She had long dark hair and wore a silver bracelet on her wrist. She lived in a framed black-and-white photograph on the wall opposite my bed and wherever I was in the room her eyes followed me with a gentle smile.

The picture had been there on my first weekend visit and over the months had become the most familiar object in the room. When I woke in the morning she was the first person I saw. In a way I could neither explain nor understand the lady was real and, somehow, my friend.

At first Aunty would only tell me that her name was Jennifer and for days I pressed her for further information. Bit by bit the story emerged. Jennifer had been their only daughter. She had been a ballerina but, at the age of twenty-one, she had hanged herself in France. Aunty asked me to forget what she'd told me and explained that she didn't like talking about Jennifer because it still upset her too much. But I'd lived with Jennifer for months. We shared the same bedroom. She was always smiling. I couldn't accept it: to me Jennifer was very much alive.

Shortly after learning about Jennifer, Uncle took me out

13

with him in the car as he visited the homes of several insurance clients. As we drove to the first house, he suggested that I might like to call Aunty and him 'Mummy' and 'Daddy'. I wasn't a bit keen on the idea and told him I'd prefer to keep things as they were. I could sense his disappointment but mummy and daddy were words which felt alien to me. I waited in the car while Uncle visited his first client and played with the locking mechanism of the driver's door. When he returned, he found himself locked out. He got pretty angry and told me to leave his door alone. At his next call I sat in the car worrying that his door might have locked itself so to make sure I checked that the door would open. Somehow I locked him out again. Uncle stood outside the car, fuming. Back home I was sent to my room with the instruction to write out a hundred times, 'I must not touch the car door locks'.

I'd been in my new home less than a month before the real confusion began. It started with Uncle coming into my room and blowing his top when he discovered me reading *The Adventures of Robin Hood*. He was furious. Why didn't I ever read any of the other books he and Aunty had bought me?

This angry outburst was just a prelude. 'What do you mean?' he shouted. 'How dare you say to Aunty that if a policeman caught you stealing he would take you away and hang you?' I didn't know how to answer – I hadn't said such a thing. It was as if Aunty and Uncle were deliberately making things up. A few days later, Uncle accused me of stealing money from the piggy bank which sat on my bedside table. The money was mine but it came out of the pocket money I was supposed to save for special occasions. I hadn't touched the money and said so, but this made Uncle even angrier. That evening, lying in bed unable to sleep, I heard the telephone ring. I heard Aunty referring to the caller as Mrs Hastings. From the way she said goodbye at the end of the conversation, I could tell she was annoyed. At breakfast I casually asked if my other Aunty Sylvia from Barkingside had called. Aunty said no, of course she hadn't. I couldn't understand why she had to lie.

In my second month in my new home, and a week before I was due to start at my new school, I was sent to my room while Aunty entertained a lady who had come to talk about me joining the local cub pack. I was hoping that Aunty would call me downstairs to meet the visitor so I could show off the silver medal I'd won at my last school's sports day. The medal was in my hand as I sat quietly listening to the murmur of voices downstairs. Half an hour must have passed before I heard a voice in my head say, 'You won't be living here much longer.'

The following Sunday morning I left the house as usual and set off for church stopping at the nearby sweet shop to buy sweets, leaving twopence out of the sixpence Aunty had given me for the collection. Walking out of the shop, I almost bumped into Uncle who seemed to be waiting for me. I watched his eyes travel down to the sweets in my hand and heard him say, 'Right, that's it. You're going back to the Village.'

I could tell from his tone of voice there would be no second chance. I was convinced that he had been looking for the first opportunity he could find to get rid of me. 'Get to church', he said coldly, 'and make sure you come straight home.' Until that moment, my feelings towards Aunty and Uncle had been vague but now I was being rejected I desperately didn't want to lose them.

The full impact of Uncle's words swept through me as I sat on the pew amongst a crowded congregation. A few people glanced curiously towards me, puzzled no doubt as to why tears were rolling down my face and why I was chewing at my nails as if possessed. I bit, oblivious of the

15

blood, until each nail was raw. I couldn't stop crying at how ugly the ends of my fingers looked. I kept seeing the pleasure on Aunty's face as she handed me the gift of a manicure set – a reward for letting my fingernails grow when I first left the Village to live with her and Uncle.

Walking the short distance back to the house I was afraid of what might be waiting for me. What names apart from thief might be flung at me. Ungrateful little child was sure to be among the descriptions. I rang the doorbell and waited. It opened slowly and standing silently behind it was Aunty. She just stood there looking at me without saying a word. Her eyes were bloodshot and filled with tears but she said nothing. She just kept on looking at me as if from a great distance. As if it was a complete stranger standing on her doorstep.

I said the first thing that came into my head: 'I'm sorry.' With a tired movement she turned her back and walked down the hall and into the kitchen. I nervously closed the door and went upstairs to my room. Uncle was obviously not home. I presumed he was playing his regular Sunday morning round of golf. About an hour later I heard Aunty walk up the stairs and say just one word: 'lunch'.

She sat opposite me at the table eating nothing, just looking at me struggling to swallow the food in front of me. I was too scared too eat and too scared not to. Her silence frightened me. I just wished she would say something, anything. Without being told, I returned upstairs to my room and listened to the silent house.

It took a week for the welfare lady to arrive and in that time the silence was broken only by terse sentences informing me a meal was ready or that it was time to have a bath and go to bed. The welfare lady came early and for most of the day held whispered conversations with Aunty and Uncle. I felt as if I didn't exist any more. As if there had

16

been a death in the house and that now all that was left was the funeral.

Late, the welfare lady came up to my room. She seemed such a kind and gentle lady I couldn't believe at first that she had come to take me away. I heard her ask me softly what things I would like to take with me and my hope that Aunty and Uncle might change their mind evaporated. Uncle walked into the room and stood there. Very quietly, with my head bowed, unable to look at his face, I said, 'I'm sorry Uncle.' In an instant his arms were around me, hugging me close to his chest. I heard him say, 'I'm sorry too.' I believed him. His arms around me, holding me for the first time, proved he really did love me but now it was too late. In that moment of realization something deep inside me exploded.

CHAPTER 4

I WASN'T SURE HOW LONG I HAD BEEN LIVING AT SHACKLEFORD House. I remembered being told that I wouldn't be returning to the Village and that I was going to a new home in Surrey. Days or weeks later I was woken up by Mr Jolliffe. 'So you're John Williams. You'll behave yourself here.' He swept past me into the dining room. The boy behind me in the breakfast queue told me that this man with thick black hair was the superintendent of the home. I was sure he had spoken to me in such an unfriendly way because he knew that I had stolen the collection money and viewed me as a thief.

Shackleford House was a large home I shared with about twenty other boys whose ages ranged from four to fifteen. Anyone over the age of eleven was designated as a senior. We juniors were dismissively referred to as 'nippers'.

During my brief stay with Aunty and Uncle I had stopped wetting the bed but at Shackleford House the habit returned with a vengeance. As a consequence I'd been allocated a bed in the room known as the nippers' bed-wetting dormitory. A little distance down the corridor was the bedroom of Mr Jolliffe's wife, a big fat lady who was rarely ever seen. I learnt that she spent a lot of time in bed suffering or recovering from various illnesses. On the rare occasions I did see her it would be to fuss over and coddle her own three children to whom the rest of the home deferred as to minor royalty.

The first thing I learned at my new school came with the nicknames I was given: 'Inky' or, sometimes, 'Rubber Lips'. In the Village and school at Barkingside nobody had ever mentioned that the colour of my skin was different. It was something I was completely unaware of. Although I disliked the daily reminder of being coloured, as the condition was politely referred to, there was one compensation. Before long I had the reputation of being the best fighter in the school. I didn't have to wrestle or punch anybody to earn this accolade. It was just assumed that being black entailed a savage strength which no one wanted to test.

There was just one other black kid at Shackleford House. Everyone, including the staff, called him by his nickname, Butch. He was a particular favourite of Mr Jolliffe's and was the only boy in the home invited into the superintendent's private flat to play with his two sons, Andrew and Gordon. From time to time Butch would fly into a violent temper, swinging his fists and screaming threats of what he would do if anyone came near him. Butch was ten, a year older than me, but in his rage he seemed to have the power of a grown man. But after these outbursts there were no recriminations. If anything they seemed to draw Butch and the superintendent even closer.

Butch went to a school close to the home while I was sent to one three miles away in Godalming. Travelling along the country roads each morning we passed the privileged halls of Charterhouse. I concentrated on sucking up to Mr Jolliffe's oldest son, Andrew, hoping desperately that if I could make him like me, his father would feel the same way.

One Saturday afternoon I was walking alone through the woods in the grounds of Shackleford House when I was

19

stopped by one of the seniors blocking the narrow path. He asked me if I would like a penny. I had just been given the sixpence weekly pocket money allowed to nine-year-olds but the offer of an extra penny was tempting nonetheless. The senior said he would give me the penny if I was 'dirty with him'. I didn't know what he meant, but agreed to follow him to his 'den'. I thought he meant one of the tree-houses some of the seniors had built but it was just a space he had cleared in the middle of some thick bracken. Not very impressed, I wondered how long it would be before he gave me the penny.

'Nobody can see us here,' said the senior as he lay down on the forest floor and pulled his long trousers down to his ankles. When his baggy white underpants came down too I knew that I wasn't going to like this game. I wanted the penny but I had never seen anything so ugly as the senior's thicket of black hair which grew up to his belly button. Worse still was the frightening thing between his legs which the senior then began to stroke. With a fascinated horror I saw how it began to swell even more. Suddenly the penny became unimportant. I wanted to be on my way to the sweet shop – sixpence was quite enough. But I couldn't just leave. Nippers had to do what seniors told them and this one was insisting that I touch the thing he was strok-ing. I couldn't do it, not for any amount of money. It was much too scary, but the senior kept insisting, begging me to do it. As he grasped my hand and pulled it towards him I began to cry. He let go when he saw me heave and go through the empty movement of vomiting.

'Touch it just once and you can go. Look I'll put this handkerchief over it first.' I thought it might bite me through the cloth but he did say I only had to touch it once. His hand took my wrist and guided my hand towards him. A momentary contact made me snatch back my hand in terror.

'Please, I want to go, I don't like it,' I said.

The senior replied with a low moan and his body began to jerk. He seemed to have lost interest in me. I thought perhaps he was feeling sick as well.

Back inside the home I made little effort to hide my distress. The cook was the first to notice, but when he asked me what was wrong I couldn't find the words to explain. He soon got irritated and dismissed me as a crybaby looking for attention. After that I knew I would have to try and forget the afternoon's events.

A few weeks later I left my bed to use the lavatory. I had to pass the open door of one of the bathrooms and, glancing inside, my eyes rested on the figure of Michael, a fourteen-year-old senior, standing naked in the bath. I couldn't stop myself from staring. The senior in the woods had been dark and hairy, the monster between his legs red and angry. But Michael's body was smooth and looked soft. Without knowing why, I was aware of a strong desire to touch his shining wet skin. He grinned at me and I forgot all about going to the toilet.

I went back to the dormitory and took from my locker some toffees I'd hoarded away. Michael was still standing there naked when I returned. I held out the toffees in my hand and said he could have them in exchange for letting me look and touch the place between his legs. He grinned again, so I said I only wanted to be dirty with him for a little while. After that I never had to offer a bribe of sweets again. In Michael's treehouse I soon mastered the sticky skill of rubbing a senior.

In the summer I went back to the Village for a week. I think someone thought it would be a good idea for me to maintain some links with the past. I stayed at the cottage I had moved to from Matron's, but I spent most of the time under suspicion of having stolen a ten shilling note from Miss Thompson's handbag. I denied all knowledge of the offence and spent the money on a wire cage and two white mice which I hid in the back garden.

Two girls in the cottage next door took a liking to me and I spent most of the week in their company, accepting their gifts of sweets and listening to them tell me how cute I was and what lovely curly hair I had. I began to worry about how I would feel when the time came to say goodbye to them but I was surprised how easy it was. By the time the welfare lady's car had passed through the village gates, the girls were little more than distant memories.

Within days of arriving back, the whole house was caught up in the excitement of packing for the annual two-week holiday. A coach arrived early one morning and by mid-afternoon both children and staff were settled in wooden huts just a few yards away from the sea at Dymchurch in Kent. On the first Saturday morning we were just finishing breakfast in the communal dining room when Mr Jolliffe stood up and told me to follow him outside. The room went silent but there was the same question on everybody's mind. What's he done wrong now? I rapidly reviewed the possibilities, which included stealing the ten-shilling note at the Village as well as defying Mr Jolliffe's instructions not to bring my two white mice to Dymchurch with me. Without saying anything, he had released them into the wild, leaving their cage on my bunk its door open. But this time I wasn't in any trouble. Stranger still, the superintendent was speaking to me in a friendly voice.

'I didn't tell you before now because you might have got a little over excited,' he said. 'In a few minutes a lady from the welfare department will be arriving to take you on a train to Wales. You are going there to meet your mother.' I'm not sure what had the most impact on me, the knowledge that somewhere in the world there existed a person who was my mum or the kindness in the superintendent's voice as he gave me the gift of such fantastic news.

As the train hurtled towards Wales I tried to picture the kind of house my mother and father lived in. I assumed I would also be meeting for the first time brothers and sisters. But I was disappointed to learn that I would be staying for a week in another Barnardo home and that my mother would be coming to visit me there. The welfare lady then handed me a letter which my mum had asked to be passed on to me. I read how sorry she was for the way things had turned out for me. Several times she wrote how much she loved me. She wanted me to know that she said a special prayer for me every night. The words themselves had little meaning to me. What affected me most was simply the tangible proof in my hand that I was the same as other children and actually had a mother of my own.

The Barnardo home in Llandudno looked out onto a busy street. On the afternoon my mum was first due to visit I positioned myself at one of the ground floor windows and scrutinized the passers-by, hoping to identify my mum before she reached the front door. Another window in a nearby room allowed me to look out onto another road, so I kept rushing from one window to the other for fear I might miss her. At one point I was convinced that a fair-haired couple with linked arms must be my parents. They looked to me just like the mum and dad I should have had. As they got nearer I heard the front door bell ring and realized I'd been standing in the wrong room. My mum had arrived and I felt a stab of nervous apprehension. I hesitated, hoping someone else would answer the door. The bell rang again. I walked towards the front door and opened it. Standing on the doorstep was a tall lady wearing a grey coat and the first thought to enter my mind was, this isn't my mum, she's a stranger come to see someone else.

'Are you John?' she asked, and almost reluctantly I nodded my head. I found myself swamped in a tight embracing hug. I felt a surge of annoyance. I was being squeezed so hard and my nose was pressed so hard against the coarse hair of the coat she was wearing that I could hardly breathe.

My feelings towards my mother improved when we arrived at the funfair on the seafront and she began dipping into her purse to pay for my tickets on the various rides. That week she came to visit me four times. Each time I asked if we could spend our time together at the fair. Between rides I was concerned with only one subject. I wanted to know everything about my father, who, I soon learned, didn't live with my mum. She said that he was a very handsome man whose home was in Africa. She had met him when he came to England to study medicine. I thought how different my life might have been if she had agreed to return home with him to Nigeria. She didn't explain why she had refused and when I learnt that my father was the son of an African chief, I became more resentful still at the ordinariness of my mother. After all, if my father was of royal blood then I, too, was a prince.

CHAPTER 5

I RETURNED TO SHACKLEFORD HOUSE WITH A NEW FEELING: I liked myself. The past was behind me and I was determined there would be no more stealing and no more reasons for Mr Jolliffe's disapproval. Now I had a mother, there was no reason for me to steal and disrupt the novel experience of feeling good. I enjoyed the emotional luxury of an easy conscience for several weeks before guilt of another kind was provoked by my discovery that hair was beginning to grow between my legs and under my arms. I observed this growth with a mixture of horror and revulsion. I felt like a freak, set apart from other children in the home. I thought I was as loathsome and ugly as the senior who had taken me into the woods to be dirty and what was happening to my body was a punishment for what had taken place that afternoon.

Feeling as guilty as a criminal I became fascinated by a murderer whose crime was front-page news – Gunther Fritz Padola who had shot and killed a policeman. I collected clippings and spent long hours imagining myself in the condemned cell waiting for execution.

All the same, I managed at last to stop wetting the bed. Mrs Jolliffe on one of her brief excursions from her room bribed me to make the effort with the offer of half a crown if I was dry for a month. I had rarely seen such a huge amount of money except when, twice a year, two elderly sisters descended on the home. Us kids would dance attendance on them for a day in the knowledge that before they left we would be formed into a queue and be solemnly handed a silver half-crown piece. I accepted Mrs Jolliffe's offer and after a couple of frustrating false starts was able to claim my reward. Unfortunately she had disappeared back to her bed and it took a while before she relented under the barrage of messages I kept sending her. I spent the entire sum on sugarlumps which, I reasoned, would last longer than sweets and thus would give me the maximum opportunity to flaunt my wealth in front of the other boys.

If tortoises have the capacity to feel shock then Percy must have suffered horribly. When I first arrived at Shackleford House, Mr Jolliffe gave permission for me to spend the money I'd brought with me on a pet rabbit but as they were in short supply that day, I came back from the shop with Percy. I wanted a pet for company and the tortoise whose head seemed permanently hidden inside his shell was a bit of a disappointment. I made a home for him in a mini glasshouse protecting a few tomato plants and, at first, fed and watered him daily. However I soon lost interest. Six months later, I remembered where I'd left Percy and returned to find him dead. His head was slumped outside his shell, his eyes missing, the sockets busy with scurrying ants. I spent the next few hours killing ants by pouring hot water on them. One of the boys asked why I was burning ants – I explained I was killing them because that's what they had done to Percy first.

When I wasn't in trouble for stealing from another boy's locker or from a desk at school, then I was a bag of nerves anticipating the punishment for losing something. Shoes, socks and bootlaces – if they belonged to me, they vanished. If there was ever a delay before a group set off for school, church, or wherever it would be caused by me searching desperately for some essential item of clothing. It was the same at school. I was always the one without a pencil to write with or who had lost the book we were supposed to be working from. What made matters worse was that I would often hide useful or important objects in a special place and then get even more confused by forgetting where that 'special place' was.

My mother came to visit me on my tenth birthday. It was a Sunday and the playroom was filled with other nippers. A lot of them tried to sit next to her and monopolize her attention. I resented the competition but also felt smug that the focus of attention was *my* mother and nobody else's. At lunchtime, Mr Jolliffe invited her into his private quarters, which didn't please me. I was sure he would turn her against me with stories of my dishonest ways. I felt that she hadn't so much been invited to lunch as summoned.

When it was time for her to leave I went in the taxi with her to Godalming station. In the back seat of the car she gave me a photograph which showed her, fishing rod in hand, a large fish dangling lifeless at the end of the line. On the station platform she told me how much she loved me. She said she wished we could be together. I promised to write to her every week, then reminded her for the last time of the promise she had made to send me a watch for Christmas. I could think of nothing I wanted quite as much, particularly if it had luminous hands which I could see in the dark. As the train disappeared, I wanted to cry but that part of me had dried up. All I could feel was a dull heavy ache. Instead of catching the bus as I'd been told to, I walked the three miles back to Shackleford House.

At school the following day the class was set the task of writing a short story. Mine was about a battle between two tribes: one good, the other bad. At the peak of the conflict the good Chief was shot down so his troops fought harder and overcame tremendous odds to win the day. The climax to my tale came with the discovery that the good Chief hadn't been killed after all, but had just been knocked unconscious. My story had quite an impact on the teacher who insisted on reading it aloud to the rest of the class. The headmaster was called in and the story was read out again. I couldn't understand why such a fuss was being made – the story had flowed so easily from my pen. As far as I was concerned I had merely written a story because the teacher had told me to.

Christmas came and with it the watch my mother had promised. For once I had in my possession something I really wanted. It made a change from the boring books and puzzles doled out by the numerous Father Christmas impersonators who visited at this time of year. The season of goodwill started early in December and continued right through January. At least twice a week we had to get dressed in Sunday suits and attend parties thrown by factory workers, the police, the navy and any other group of individuals moved to charity. Worse still, we had to write letters afterwards saying how much we had enjoyed the party and the presents we had received. In truth by the 25th I was sick and tired of being a professional party guest but the arrival of the watch made it feel like Christmas should really be. For the first time I felt warmth and affection for my mother. She had sent me exactly what I wanted and that Christmas night I spent hours awake under my blankets on my bed absorbed by the luminous numbers and hands. The green glow, beating like a human heart, for once lifted my usual fear of being alone and vulnerable in the dark.

On Boxing Day afternoon I turned the winder of my watch past the point of no return. There was an awful angry buzzing sound as both hands raced round the dial at a furious pace and then stopped dead. At first I didn't believe what I had done. I tried turning the winder again, shaking the watch, but still it laid lifeless in my hand. I wanted to burst into tears but I was afraid of alerting anyone to what I had just done: my most treasured possession was broken and useless.

In the short time I'd owned the watch I had showed it proudly to almost everyone in the home so I knew I wouldn't be able to keep what I'd done secret for long. The guilt I felt was bad enough but the humiliation of exposure would be unbearable. Somehow I had to shift the blame. One of the nippers was lying stretched full-length on the playroom floor assembling a plastic model. I pretended to stumble over his feet and then accused him of making me drop the watch in my hand but it was a waste of time. The nipper flatly refused to accept any blame and I walked away with an even keener sense of my destructiveness.

A frequent visitor to the home was a man we called Uncle Bob. I told him about my watch and he took it away, promising to get it repaired. Each time he returned to the home he came with a story why he didn't have the watch with him: it was still at the repair shop; he'd left it on the mantlepiece at home; he would bring it with him next week. I wanted to believe him but after several weeks he was beginning to remind me of the couple who had taken me out for the day and had said they would return the following week but never did. After three months I gave up hope of seeing my watch again. In a few days the occupants of Shackleford House would be moving to Eastbourne in Sussex where the staff and boys were to merge with another Barnado home called Churchill House. On the day we climbed aboard the coach to our new home I knew that my watch was lost forever.

CHAPTER 6

THE NEW HOME WAS MUCH LIKE THE OLD. THERE WERE NEW faces to get used to living with but the rules were still the same and Mr Jolliffe was still in charge. At my new school, St Mark's, at least some things were new. A bright blue rosette was pinned to the blazer of the boy judged to be the most smartly dressed every Monday morning. I longed to win the prize and wear the rosette for a week, and after several attempts I managed to do so. I was pleased but any sense of triumph was dulled by my suspicion I had won first prize purely because of my regularity in standing in the line-up.

My mother stopped writing her weekly letters when I moved to Churchill House. It wasn't until several months had passed that I realized we had lost contact with each other. One Saturday morning, I was sat on a swing near the sand pit when I heard a voice in my head say, 'You're on your own now and that's how it's always going to be.' I wasn't concerned. The voice had simply confirmed what I already knew in my heart.

On another Saturday morning I walked with Alan, another boy from the home, into the nearby village of Ocklynge. At the end of a narrow street was a shop I often visited which sold musical instruments. If I could have chosen anything from the window display it would have been the silver mouth-organ on the red velvet stand. The thief in me had noted on previous visits that there was rarely anyone behind the counter and that morning I told Alan that the old lady who owned the shop must be upstairs in her flat so I was going to sneak inside and nick the mouth-organ. I slipped inside while he kept watch and in seconds was behind the counter sliding back the glass panel which protected the goods in the window. The mouth-organ was in easy reach and, concealing it down my shirt, I left the shop and walked smartly up the street with Alan close behind. We had gone a few yards when a shout made us both turn our heads – it was the old lady. We both began to run and turned down a side alley which unfortunately led to a dead end. Turning back, we found our escape blocked by a group of irate local shopkeepers.

Alan began wailing like a baby as soon as the policeman locked us in the back of his car. The constable didn't need to ask where we lived and announced he was taking us back to the home. Alan's cries got louder as he begged the policeman to let him go. I sat next to him very quietly. I'd never been in such serious trouble and I wasn't looking forward to facing Mr Jolliffe. As the police car swept up the drive and stopped in front of the home's main door I saw the windows fill with curious excited faces. Mr Jolliffe's face had an expression I couldn't read. He told us to stand with our faces to the wall inside the front hall while he and the policeman held a short conversation. On previous occasions I'd faced Mr Jolliffe's anger in the front office. This time he told Alan and me to follow him and the constable along the corridor of his private quarters and sat us down in his sitting room. If I hadn't been in trouble I would have felt privileged to be there. Mr Jolliffe seemed unusually benign and sat, saying very little, as the policeman asked for an account of what had happened and wrote in his notebook.

The policeman's questions took only a few minutes to answer. When he had finished, he closed his notebook, glanced at Mr Jolliffe and rose from his chair. Mr Jolliffe, trying to impress upon the policeman the general honesty of the children in his care, turned to me before showing the constable out and said,

'None of the other children have ever stolen from shops, have they?' It was a question he shouldn't have asked: for the past few weeks a shoplifting craze had been rife in the home. Without thinking I replied,

'Oh yes, lots of them have,' and I volunteered the names of a couple of boys in the home.

'Go and get them,' thundered Mr Jolliffe, and the policeman sat down again. An hour later, Mr Jolliffe's sitting room was filled with at least a dozen other guilty shoplifters.

Even on holiday I was unable to keep out of trouble. A heavy atmosphere of suspicion settled over the camp at Dymchurch where the home was once again staying for the two-week summer vacation. A catering pack containing fifty chocolate Penguin bars had gone missing from the stores. For once I presented an effective alibi so, despite my previous history, avoided being accused.

After a couple of days I was confident I was in the clear, but I'd reckoned without the guile of Mrs Jolliffe. She called me one afternoon into the trailer caravan she was staying in, gave me a cup of tea and asked if I was happy. She wanted to know what sort of things I was interested in and what I would like to do when I was old enough to leave school. It was the longest conversation I'd ever had with her. I thought she was kind and very nice. When she asked if it had been me who had stolen the chocolate biscuits and assured me it would be just between the two of us, I couldn't lie and told her it was me. I explained where I had buried them and she asked me to go and dig them up for her. I should have known better – within hours everybody in the home knew who the culprit was and I was back on punishment.

To make matters worse I'd also confessed to Mrs Jolliffe about stealing money from the till of a nearby baker's shop. I'd slipped behind the counter after asking for warm bread rolls, which had to be fetched from the back kitchen. With part of the three pounds I'd stolen I bought a crab from the fishmongers. I carried it back to the camp site and claimed I had caught the dangerous looking beast in the sea. The cook pointed out that the crab's colour meant it had already been boiled. I changed my story to having found the crab on the beach. My attempt to impress ended up in the pigswill bin. As punishment for stealing the chocolate biscuits and the money from the bakery I was confined to the camp while the rest of the home were taken on a trip to the funfair but as soon as they left I squeezed through a narrow window in Mrs Jolliffe's caravan and helped myself to a handful of silver coins which were left in the pocket-money tray.

My secondary school education began at Bishop Bell Church of England school. Mine was the only black face amongst six hundred pupils. The two other black kids in the home went to other schools in the town, which suited me fine. The last thing I needed was the reflection of another black face at school. In fact the colour of my skin was copper-brown and I cringed whenever I heard the word used in any context. To be black was an inferior condition. If I caught sight of one of the West Indian railway staff at the station I felt a mixture of superiority and contempt. Somehow I was able to both hate and deny the colour of my skin. I found it similar in shade to the unpleasant smelling turds which floated in the water of the toilet pan.

Few lessons at school held any interest for me other than religious studies. Whenever we moved between class-rooms for different subjects I would search the desk I was sitting at for something worth stealing or something to read. I would keep half an ear on what the teacher was saying and could usually bluff my way if challenged. I was a lot happier at school than at Churchill House. I had no shortage of friends there and soon emerged as the leader of the class. My popularity and status grew when I won the inter-form cross-country race and went on to become Eastbourne's junior schoolboy champion. The day after the race, my picture appeared in the local paper. At school, the headmaster congratulated me publicly and six hundred pairs of hands applauded my achievement. There was no reaction at all at Churchill House. I got back late after the race and stood in the empty dining room, tears running down my face because nobody was interested.

My friends at school loved visiting me at the Home and were always included in the events organized every evening, perhaps a football match or a game of pirates in the basement gymnasium. I would have liked to visit them in their homes, but never mentioned it. The lack of invitations didn't result from malice or selfishness but, in comparison to the organized games they enjoyed at Churchill House, they must have imagined I would find their homes boring. During the few hours they spent with the Barnado boys and their various friends from other schools they couldn't see the bickering and jealousy which dominated the emotional environment of the home.

Relationships in the home were basically feudal, descending in order of preference from the throne on which the Jolliffe family sat. Next in line came the staff. The pecking order of the children was based primarily on age. One of the worst possible offences was for a boy to attempt to forge a relationship with a member of staff. We were all constantly on the watch and ready with accusations of brownnosing, crawling, sucking up.

I did have one good friend in the home but I lost him at the beginning of my second year at Bishop Bell. John O'Dell had come to Shackleford House shortly after me. He was a year younger than me and in the early days I'd taken it upon myself to look after him and show him around. Since then we had been close friends. Whenever I was in trouble I could always count on his friendship but this came to a halt on the day John started at the local grammar school. We were walking downstairs to the breakfast room when Mr Jolliffe emerged from another landing. He saw us together and said to John, 'Now that you're going to grammar school, I wouldn't have anything more to do with him.' Meaning me. He underlined his opinion of me by announcing after prayers that in future nobody was to swop anything with me because I was dishonest and would trick anyone given the slightest excuse. He was referring to one of the boys who made a deal with me then changed his mind and complained he'd been swindled. John should have walked with me to the bus-stop that morning, but he made in excuse and left early.

I lost a friend at the home, but at school that day I became fascinated by one of the new boys. Ian had come to Bishop Bell from junior school with the reputation of being a brilliant footballer. I listened as some of my friends praised his skills and as soon as I saw him I thought he was everything I really wanted to be. Over a period of weeks my interest became almost an obsession. If he came near me, smiled or said hello I'd feel my face beginning to burn. I found it impossible to be natural with him. Once he grabbed hold of me playfully in a bear hug, placing his cheek next to mine as he squeezed. I didn't want him to let go and I could feel his arms round me for days. Watching him from a distance, thinking about him all day, troubled me. I couldn't understand why he reduced me to a stammer when we spoke but I knew that my feelings had to be kept secret. I was convinced the emotions he provoked in me were bad. If he ever guessed how he made me feel I was sure he would look at me with contempt.

CHAPTER 7

IT NEVER OCCURRED TO ME THAT MY INTEREST IN THE NEW BOY was sexual. Sex was something dirty and secret. A boy in my year had been caught trousers-down with a first year in the art room cupboard. The whole school learnt about it but I was the one who led the chants of 'Homo! Homo!' whenever one of the two boys' names was mentioned – pulling down boys' trousers was something I kept confined to Churchill House.

What had started with a tin of toffees to bribe Michael had grown to a regular number of boys who were willing to let me wank them off. I was also growing aware that there were grown-ups who were interested in what lay hidden inside underpants . . .

Sunday evening was bathtime, in preparation for school the next day. It was also the regular house mother's off-duty period. We all knew that another, male, staff member would be supervising the baths. I always felt embarrassed by the way insisted on standing me up in the bath and leaned close while he scrupulously washed between my legs with the flannel. The discomfort was increased by the presence of another boy in the adjacent bath who could see me standing naked. When he was satisfied with his work he would move on to the next boy, but he wasn't content with simply washing us. He would then tell us to wait in the bath until he was ready to towel us dry.

One evening, when this stand-in supervisor had left for another bathroom, promising to return, I felt an unfamiliar surge of defiance. Without permission I got out of the bath, dried myself and was just putting on my shoes when he reappeared. I could sense his anger and that in itself seemed to me a small victory. That evening, after all the other boys had been bathed, I stood at the front of the noisy chattering supper queue outside the kitchen. Suddenly he appeared and shouted for silence. I didn't stop laughing quickly enough and felt something smash hard into my face. Too shocked to feel the pain, my eyes filled with tears. My nose felt as big as an orange and blood poured from it as if from a tap, soaking my tee-shirt. My attacker's rage evaporated. He rushed me into the kitchen and held my head over a sink. From the tone of his voice and the way he was gently applying a cold compress above my nose I knew he was afraid he had gone too far. I wasn't going to cry: for once, someone else had done something wrong so I was in a position of power.

Refusing to cry was also my response to corporal punishment. The staff had long since given up shouting at me and resorted to six strokes of the cane instead. Sometimes they dispensed with the formality of the stick and would bounce me round the walls of an office with a mixture of punches and slaps, and afterwards they would examine the expression on my face, looking for signs of tears. What they saw instead was detached impassiveness. I wouldn't cry for them, but later I would find a quiet corner and sob. Tears were dangerous – they brought with them helplessness.

In my third year at Bishop Bell I became aware of friends in my class taking an interest in girls. We had been through several crazes like conker fighting, marbles and card flicking but now it was girls and I felt left behind. The craze I'd felt most involved in was the wrestling game which included a mandatory grope of the opponent's crutch. It was all done with a sense of fun, laughing and giggling as we struggled to size each other up. There was no sense of doing anything wrong, it was just another game. The real queers hid away in places like the art cupboard and the venom for them remained. Indeed with the increase in interest in girls, the abuse became more virulent. I felt compelled to lead the chorus of taunts – I couldn't let anyone know how much the naked bodies of my friends excited me. Girls held no interest for me however much I discussed the size of their tits and which girls would be easiest to feel up.

There were to be changes too at Churchill House. Mr Jolliffe was leaving to take over the running of another home some fifty miles away. It was the best news I'd ever heard having lived in fear of him so long. It took a while to believe he really was going.

Nobody in the home could have watched his preparations for leaving more closely than me. Each time a load of his personal effects was driven away I felt more relieved and excited. The day before his official departure I crept into his private rooms. There were still a few packing cases waiting for collection. From one not properly sealed I stole three Bible-shaped money boxes. The names of his children were embossed on the cover in gold. Careless of discovery, even wanting Mr Jolliffe to know, I forced the lock on each box and pocketed the money. Now he had almost gone I wanted Mr Jolliffe to know how much I hated him.

The Jolliffes were replaced by the Catternachs, a middle-aged couple who always dressed as if about to attend a society wedding. They soon upset the rest of the staff by encouraging the children to visit them in their private quarters whenever they felt like watching television or just for a chat. The Catternachs wanted to create an informal family atmosphere but the staff preferred the more rigid regime of the Jolliffes. I was the first to accept the Catternachs' invitation and spent most of my free time with them, ignoring the accusations of crawling.

One Saturday morning a luxury coach swept up the main drive and we were loaded on board to be driven to a charity cricket match being played between the touring West Indian side and a local team. I wasn't particularly interested in the game but with the money I'd stolen from the Jolliffes' flat I'd bought a camera and I wanted to take some pictures of Gary Sobers. He was in a fielding position close to the boundary facing away from me but in a lull between overs he turned and smiled as I snapped several shots. There was a big crowd at the match and I spent some time wandering amongst the people gathered round the ice-cream vans and beer tents. Standing on his own I saw an enormously fat little boy about six years old eating an ice-cream. I thought to myself what a fatty he would grow up to be. He noticed me staring and pulled a face. I responded by poking my tongue at him.

During the lunch interval I sat in the stands watching the motor roller driving up and down the wicket flattening the bumps and scuff marks the players had made. I could see the fat boy waddling beside the roller and laughing with the man driving the machine. I turned my head for a moment then felt a wave of shock sweep through the stands. The fat boy had fallen and the roller had crushed him. Four grown-ups picked him from the ground and ran awkwardly cradling his body. A voice over the loud-speaker system asked if there was a doctor in the stadium but people were saying that the boy was dead. It was impossible for him to survive the massive injuries to his head. I started to shake. I was convinced that I was responsible for his death.

That night, lying in the dark dormitory, the sleeping boys looked to me like shrouded corpses. I couldn't erase from my mind the hostile looks the fat boy and I had exchanged shortly before his death. The last person to look at him with scorn had been me. I was sure he would return from the beyond the grave with vengeance on his mind. Unable to stand the intense fear I got out of my bed and risked waking one of the staff. I explained that I had been woken by a nightmare. She put on a dressing gown and sat on my bed for a couple of minutes whispering reassurance before returning to her room. As soon as she left, the terror came flooding back. I couldn't bother her again. I could only pray that morning would soon come. The Sunday newspapers carried a report of the cricket match as well as the boy's death. To make matters worse, I learnt that it had been the fat boy's grandfather driving the roller. A few hours later he too had been found dead. He had taken his own life.

There was a girl in my class at school called Patricia. She had long dark hair, a chubby body and breasts of a grown woman pushing through her navy blue jumper. I knew from her friends that Pat had a crush on me so in order to conceal my attraction to other boys from my mates, I asked her out for a date. Mr Catternach seemed amused when I asked for a pocket-money advance to take Pat to the pictures and as it was to be my first date he gave me ten shillings from his own pocket. I met Pat as arranged on a Saturday afternoon and suggested we go to the Odeon where the X-rated film *Lolita* was showing. Because I thought it was the correct adult thing to do, I led her to the back row where other couples were already snogging. I felt miserably uncomfortable sitting holding her hand. Holding hands felt soft and stupid. I knew that eventually I would have to kiss her and I was dreading that. I tried to concentrate on the film but it didn't make much sense.

The only thing I could grasp was that an old man wanted a young girl's body.

When the end credits began to roll I turned clumsily and met Pat's waiting lips. I kissed her in the way I had seen it done on the screen. I could feel her breasts straining towards me. I thought about placing my hand there but realized I didn't know how to touch them. The house lights came up and I was relieved the date was almost over. All that was left to do was walk her to the bus-stop, kiss her on the cheek and wave goodbye.

By Monday morning my feelings for Pat had shifted from indifference to dislike. When she walked towards me in the playground with a smile on her face, I immediately assumed she was laughing at me, that she knew how sexually inept I was with girls. Without explanation I turned my back on her and walked quickly away. For the next twelve months I completely ignored her. Her friends often asked what she had done wrong but the only answer I could give was, 'I don't like her.' Sitting in the classroom it felt as if her eyes were always on me, watching and hoping I would relent. The puzzlement mixed with an expression of pain on her face only fuelled my resentment. Her face seemed to signal 'I still like you'. This made me feel even angrier. How could she be so stupid?

The hurt I caused Pat and the way I usually led the verbal attacks on others didn't bother me. The opposite applied if ever I witnessed an adult in any form of emotional distress. Butch, the other black kid in the home and the favourite of Mr Jolliffe, took an instant dislike for a new member of staff. The spiteful words he hissed often reduced her to tears and for some reason this deeply disturbed me. I could hardly bear to witness such open expression of grief. I bribed Butch with sweets just to leave her alone and not make her cry. A new teacher arrived at school and within days the entire class was aware how easy it was to bring him too the verge of frustrated tears. Each jibe and taunt thrown at him seemed to strike me. The teacher must have realized I was one of the few never to take the mickey out of him. At times I thought he recognized the pity in my eyes.

One afternoon he hit back and, to my astonishment, called me out to the front of the class. He said he'd had enough of all the cheek and was going to make an example of me. The four vicious swipes with the cane stung but not as much as my feeling of humiliation and betrayal.

At Churchill House the antagonism directed at the Catternachs by the staff was getting worse. Us kids were being encouraged to take sides by adopting an attitude of non-co-operation. One evening as I was leaving the Catternachs' flat and bracing myself for the inevitable snide remarks about where I had been, Mrs Catternach told me she and her husband would soon be leaving. She wanted me to be the first to know as she appreciated I had been one of their most loyal supporters. She went on to suggest if someone was to write to head office explaining the children didn't want them to leave, that they were being forced to, something might be done about it. She added it might be a good idea if the person who wrote the letter made a point of saying how good she and her husband had been to the children.

I wrote the letter almost immediately and finished it by saying that if Barnado's was really a Christian organization they couldn't allow the unfairness to the Catternachs to continue. A few days later an official from head office arrived. He spent much of the day with the staff then came to speak to me. I repeated the points in my letter emphasizing it wasn't right that the new people were being forced to leave.

'Nobody is forcing them to leave,' he said. 'They handed

in their resignations some time ago. Under the circumstances I can see no way of persuading them to stay.' I felt as if I'd been used. Their suggestion that someone write to head office seemed to have arisen out of their wish to be seen as blameless, not because intervention might enable them to stay on.

After the Catternachs' departure a former housemaster came to take over. He had left the home a few years earlier to work in an isolated part of the country as a member of a search-and-rescue team saving people lost or injured on the bleak and hostile terrain.

The staff seemed content with Mr Brown's arrival. We kids were soon won over by the way he talked and listened to us as individuals. Sometimes we'd discuss between us how he could get us to do what he wanted without raising his voice or threatening punishment. The closest we came to an answer was that we liked him. Though I couldn't pin down exactly why, I thought him mysterious. His face and the sandals he wore on his feet reminded me of the picture of Jesus hanging in the main hall. When his eyes rested on mine I was sure he saw clearly the things I disliked about myself, yet there would still be a twinkling in his eyes and a smile on his face.

One of the oldest children at fourteen, I'd landed the job of making early morning tea for extra pocket money. I'd get out of bed an hour before the rest of the home and take tea in bed to each member of staff. I always felt sad for Mr Brown when I reached his flat: I couldn't understand why such a nice man had so very few possessions. Every morning I'd knock gently on his bedroom door and heard him call for me to leave his tea in the kitchen. He didn't even want the luxury of a hot cup of tea in bed.

Mr Brown changed the usual venue of the home's summer holiday and took us to the New Forest in Hampshire. We were all excited by the wild but friendly ponies roaming round the tents searching for food but I had another reason too. I could hardly wait until it was time to settle down for the night in our sleeping bags. By a mutual but unspoken consent I would be sleeping next to Jeff. He was thirteen and over the previous few weeks I'd noticed how, his eyes like my own were continually glancing down at other boys' crutches.

The two boys sleeping at the other end of the tent couldn't see how close together Jeff and I were lying. There was a conversation about what might happen tomorrow, and much laughter and joking between the four of us. Best of all, under the cover of darkness my hand had slipped into the opening of Jeff's sleeping bag and was gently rubbing his cock. For the five years I'd spent giving wanks to seniors, I'd never allowed them to touch me in the same way. So when Jeff's hand began moving down my body I was surprised at how pleasurable it felt. I wasn't scared of him. He was younger than me. We shared something in common I'd been ashamed of: the growth of hair between our legs. For the first time, I felt my hand exploring other parts of a boy's body. I wanted to do more than rub a cock. I wanted to picture what couldn't be seen in the dark and match it to the delicious sensation of touching warm velvet skin.

When Jeff and the others in the tent had fallen asleep I began touching myself imagining it was Jeff's hand. Then I started rubbing and tensing my body just as I'd seen so many seniors do. Suddenly the most exquisitely sweet feeling took over my whole body and mind and I knew this was the tickling feeling I'd heard so much about. I was impatient to repeat the experience but, never having known anything but a set time for meals, school and bed, I naturally assumed I would have to wait until the same time the following night. It was a long time to wait but there was compensation. I had discovered

45

at last a foolproof method of making myself feel good.

Those two weeks in the New Forest were the best holiday of my life. From then on I abandoned any other interests I had, such as car spotting or playing the piano, to concentrate on sex. Sex was about getting to see a boy with a hard on, bringing him by hand to an orgasm and letting him do the same to me. Robert, a stocky fair-haired boy, had slipped away with me from a football game in the gym one evening and we hid ourselves away in the sick bay which wasn't being used at the time. Outside the light was fading but we could still see clearly enough to rush through a game of strip poker which left us both conveniently naked. We'd been lying on one of the beds for a few minutes when we heard the sound of footsteps moving down the corridor towards us. We grabbed hold of our clothes and dived under the bed but made too much noise. The lights went on and one of the house mothers was crouching down demanding we come out from where we were trying to hide. She didn't believe for one moment the excuse we were playing cards. 'In the dark? With no clothes on?' she questioned indignantly. 'Get dressed and go to your dormitories.' As she followed us along the corridor she let us know what dirty little boys we were. 'And don't think Mr Brown won't be hearing about this,' she added.

I didn't sleep much that night, waking up with the fear that it wouldn't be long before everyone in the home knew I was a homo, a queer. There were boys with a score to settle, like Chris. We travelled to school together and were in the same class. I had given him the nickname Weird which stuck for more than four years. He'd just started going after girls and was bound to tell everyone at school about what had happened in the sick bay. The new term and my final year at Bishop Bell was due to start in a few days. I wasn't looking forward to it one bit.

The next morning we hid ourselves in the loft above the shed where the pet rabbits were caged. We talked about what might happen but as there was little we could do we took our minds off things by continuing with our interrupted wanking session. Mr Brown sent word he wanted to see us separately in the afternoon. There were only the three of us in the house as the rest of the Home had been taken for a walk across the downs. I knocked on the door to his flat at two o'clock and was ushered into his sitting room. He wasn't angry or disgusted as I had expected. On the table was tea and biscuits for two. I got a little embarrassed when he asked for details about what we were actually doing with our clothes off but, apart from that, he only seemed interested in discovering the names of any other boys I'd had sex with. Before leaving his flat he said that what I'd been caught doing wasn't really wrong but was best avoided. Patting me on the shoulder he assured me that the previous night's events were to be regarded as confidential. I had nothing to fear about being exposed.

CHAPTER 8

AT FIFTEEN I WAS OLD ENOUGH TO LEAVE SCHOOL AND Churchill House. For weeks I'd been looking forward to the end of the spring term and living in the outside world. Instead of reading books during lessons I wrote down on scraps of paper the financial details of my future lifestyle. I imagined a two-bedroomed flat overlooking the sea and carpeted throughout in a deep red pile. I expected to find a job which would pay at least five pounds a week. This would be more than enough, I thought, to cover the rent and pay for the electric guitar which would launch my pop-singing career. I forgot to budget for food, but made neat little columns of figures itemizing other extras such as the telephone and drinks for the cocktail cabinet.

At three o'clock on the final day at school we left the class as a group and made our way to the assembly hall for the last time for the headmaster's farewell address. The following Monday I was to start work as a kitchen assistant. The wage would be four pounds and ten shillings. School had become even more irrelevant. In a few days I could even choose what time I went to bed.

On the way to the assembly hall I darted into the toilets. The distant sound of hymn singing signalled the coast was clear and I was running down the corridor and out into the playground. I expected to hear the shout of a teacher telling me to stop but even if I had I wouldn't have taken any notice. Sprinting along the road which took me away from school I thought my days of being told what to do were finally over.

Where I was going to live? Eastbourne was a holiday town and most of the rented accommodation was for short-stay guests. The Barnardo welfare officer as a last resort arranged lodgings for me a few miles away at Hailsham. I wasn't too pleased. Butch had been placed there for a while and he was continually on the phone to Mr Brown to say how unhappy he was. Eventually he came back to Churchill House for a few weeks before becoming a junior soldier with the army which Mr Rose the welfare officer also suggested as a career for me. He thought Barnardo boys were particularly suited to the discipline of military life. I said I wasn't keen. What I really would have liked was to work in a film studio.

I left Churchill House after my first week's work squeezing jam into doughnuts and spreading chocolate over biscuits. Only two people were around to say good-bye. The boy with whom I was having a farewell wanking session when the welfare officer arrived and Mr Brown, who walked out to the car with me and waved as I was driven away.

It only took me a few hours to realize the life I'd imagined for myself in the classroom was not going to happen immediately. The council house and the small bedroom my new landlady showed me to felt tiny and oppressive compared to the familiar sprawling expanse of Churchill House.

I unpacked the clothes provided by Barnardo's and went downstairs to be introduced to the seventeen-year-old daughter who was drinking tea with her mother in the kitchen. Neither of them smiled and in a roundabout fashion they made it clear they would prefer not to have to take in lodgers. Before going back to my room I was told I could have a bath on Wednesdays and Sundays. The daughter said I could do with one now and what an awful smell I brought into their house from my work in the teashop.

I stayed there until the following Saturday. I was up early to catch the bus into Eastbourne and was eating cornflakes when I noticed the sealed envelope on the kitchen table. It was addressed to the landlady's son who was due back home on leave from the army. I'd heard all about him in between monologues from the landlady describing her day at work as an auxiliary nurse. From the way she went on she gave the impression she was at least a consultant surgeon. Sure that the letter would have something to say about me, I opened it. I was right. There was an apology that another coloured boy from the homes had taken over his room and an explanation that it wouldn't have happened if she hadn't needed the extra money so badly. At Churchill House there had been occasions when an older boy had run away only to return a few days later but it had never entered my mind to abscond because I had nowhere else to go. But this letter convinced me that I wasn't wanted and that I would have to find another place to live. I went back upstairs packed my clothes back into my suitcase and left the house for good.

By the time the bus I was on reached Eastbourne I had decided what to do. A few months before, I had spent a weekend in Brighton with one of the boys from the home at his mother's house. I remembered her saying I was always welcome to visit so I caught a train and knocked on her door. Mrs Carrick was very understanding. I explained why I had left my lodgings and she said I could stay in her small basement flat until I was able to find somewhere more suitable. The welfare officer called a week later and didn't seem a bit surprised at what had happened. He said he'd return in a couple of weeks and if in the meantime I found other lodgings he'd see what he could do about subsidising any rent I had to pay.

I stayed with Mrs Carrick for a month but I think she was quite relieved when I found alternative accommodation a few streets away. I don't think she had realized just how unpractical and incompetent I was at looking after myself. We had agreed that when I found work I would pay her two pounds a week for food and other expenses. I soon got a job as an apprentice sugar boiler in a sweet factory but on Friday evenings with my wages in my pocket I would go out and spend the lot, returning penniless and expecting Mrs Carrick to keep me through the following week. My next landlady was a tiny thin woman who lived with her equally tiny husband, a solicitor's clerk. The welfare officer met them both before I moved in and discussed how the shortfall in my wages could be made up to cover my boarding costs.

I wasn't happy. I couldn't stop thinking about Churchill House and the people I'd left behind in Eastbourne. Walking the streets to work and back I searched for my friends from the past in the faces of boys on bicycles, in buses and on foot. I thought that if I could make even one friend the loneliness would vanish. I spotted lots of boys I instinctively wanted to talk to, but I couldn't bring myself to smile or say 'hello' because I was afraid they might guess that my friendship entailed a need to undress.

My loneliness was accompanied by a permanent hunger. My small frail landlady served the same amount of food to me as she and her husband were content with. At the end of the evening meal she would ask, as if challenging me, 'Have you had enough?' Not wanting to offend, I would always say yes, thank you. Once I had paid for my lodgings I had thirty shillings to last me for the week. It wasn't enough to do much more than buy extra food and sweets so I spent a lot of my spare time sitting on a wooden bench in the nearby cemetery: I was drawn to the place. It was a sanctuary where I could escape from my unhappiness and indulge my urge to pack my bags and run away to France where I pictured sunshine and picking grapes in a vineyard all day. I had never been abroad. At school geography had been a subject I found even more boring than most but when I sat in the graveyard, a wish to travel began to develop.

The next time the welfare officer came to visit I told him that I wanted to join the merchant navy. He said he had contacts and after I'd filled in the necessary forms I could expect to wait about three months before leaving for sea-training school. In the meantime I left the sweet factory for a better paid job which had a tenuous link to the world of film. The ad in the paper said a photographic studio was looking for a young man to assist with developing and printing. I thought the job promised the glamour of the showbiz world I so badly wanted but for most of the day I was cramped into a dark cubby hole unrolling film after film of family snapshots that came in from all over the country. As the youngest member of the small workforce it was my job to walk to the post office every morning to collect the latest batch of film. It occurred to me that some people were bound to send cash instead of cheques or postal orders, so on the way back from the post office I'd make a series of lucky dips into the bag to supplement my wages.

The mailbag ruse was a hit-and-miss affair and my room at the lodging house had rolls of film secreted all over it. A more regular source of income came from my landlady's bedroom where I discovered a box in which she kept notes and silver. Whenever I needed a couple of pounds for a ring-side seat at the wrestling or a trip to the pictures I

52

helped myself. I thought if I only took a bit at a time it wouldn't be missed. The box was almost empty when the landlady demanded to know why I'd been stealing from her. I denied all knowledge but she wasn't convinced and said she was phoning for the welfare officer to get me moved somewhere else. There was a possibility I might have to return to Churchill House. I couldn't face the shame of that so, as soon as the landlady's back was turned, I left the house and walked down to the sea-front.

I had enough money for one night in a cheap bed-and-breakfast place. I objected when the proprietor showed me to a room with twin beds but he said I wasn't to worry as the other bed wasn't intended for use . . . Satisfied I had a roof over my head for at least one night, I left to spend the rest of the day in a cinema. When I returned to the room it was obvious that someone else had been moved in.

I was annoyed, felt I was being taken advantage of. I was also afraid of spending the night in a room with a stranger. I didn't ask for my money back but took with me as I left a multi-channel transistor radio sitting amongst the other person's belongings on the bed. I walked back to the sea-front and hid under a sheet of tarpaulin covering a stack of neatly folded deck-chairs. It was just getting light when the beam of a torch lit up the cave I had made for myself. It was a policeman. 'Hello,' he said in a friendly tone, 'we've been looking everywhere for you. We were really worried.'

I couldn't believe how kindly people spoke to me. I was in the police station because I'd stolen things but nobody made me feel as if I'd done anything wrong. A policeman in civilian clothes asked where I'd got the radio from. He was also curious where I'd got all the rolls of film he'd found in my room. He seemed like such a nice man I told him everything. Later that day I was left in a room with a scruffily dressed tramp. The constable had said he'd be back for me in a moment but he was beaten to it by the detective who'd been speaking to me earlier. He was furious.

'How dare you leave this child on his own with an adult. Is there no sense in that thick head of yours?' The constable blushed bright red and hurried the tramp out. The detective then explained he'd be taking me in his car to a remand home a few miles outside of Brighton. He assured me I would like it there. I did. It was what I was most familiar with: a large rambling house set in its own grounds and filled with lots of boys. Even better than Churchill House was the knowledge I was living with other thieves. I felt safe for the first time since leaving Eastbourne.

CHAPTER 9

THE HOUSE OF THE TREES PROBATION HOME LOOKED DOWN over terraces of cottages like a mining valley in South Wales. Set high on the side of the hill it looked like the sort of place where the local squire would once have lived but had now been taken over by the Salvation Army. The present master was Captain Tribble. He actually lived with his wife and three children in a building adjacent to the main house and it was there the probation officer who had driven me from Brighton first took me. The Captain, who preferred to be called Skip, was a tubby man in his early fifties. His round red face showed few signs of strain or stress. A very obedient golden labrador followed us into the office and lay comfortably on the carpet as if to listen to what his master had to say.

There was good news and not so good news. First, said Skip, I'd been fortunate enough to join the twenty or so other boys at the home. There had been several other possible candidates with dark skin but to avoid bullying it was Skip's policy to only ever have one coloured boy at a time. He'd also spoken to the rest of the boys at morning prayers to alert them to my arrival and to warn that punishment would follow any incidence of name-calling.

The not so good news was passed on by Skip's wife who

said she liked everybody to call her mum. I thought not likely, but listened as she explained that a shortage of bed space meant I'd have to spend a few weeks sleeping in the bed-wetter's dorm. It was nearly suppertime so I followed Skip and the dog into the main house to be introduced to the lads waiting in the dining room.

I got to meet the rest of the staff at breakfast. They sat together at a highly polished trestle table from where they listened with the rest of the room to a bible reading, prayers and Skip's final announcements. His immediate deputies were lieutenants Mr and Mrs Ray. He was an even more roly-poly version of Skip wearing a baggy matted jersey. His wife didn't seem to smile very much but she was who you saw if you were sick. The three civilians at the table supervised the home's working activities. Mr Walsh ran the poultry and market garden, Mr Lord – or Jock behind his back – the woodwork shop with Tuesday nights as scoutmaster and an even fatter man called Cryer was in charge of the farm party. The farm was where Skip decided I would be put to work.

I soon settled in but I loathed going to work on the farm. It was starting to get very cold and young men working hard on the farm milking cows or slopping out pig shit didn't need such luxuries as gloves, fatty Cryer would tease. Skip believed in an early start to the day. He called us from warm beds at five-thirty to shake the sleep from our eyes with a half-mile run round the grounds. The next stop was the wash house for a cold shower and permission was given to dry and get dressed when he judged each boy had stood under the icy jet for long enough. For those of us unlucky enough to be on early milking it was then out to the cowshed until breakfast.

During my time at the remand home I'd asked the Barnardo welfare officer who came to visit if he could put me back in touch with my mother. In November a letter from her arrived at the House of the Trees. I began reading and resentfully decided it could have been the first one I'd ever received more than six years previously. I didn't want to hear again how sorry she was. I wanted a mother who was strong and could make me feel what it would be like to be her son.

I did reply to a couple of her letters but then lost interest.

I'd never completely lost touch with Aunty Sylvia whose house I used to visit from the Village at Barkingside. One of Skip's rules was a compulsory letter home at weekends and I began writing to her regularly. She didn't forget my birthday. A brightly covered parcel arrived crammed with chocolate and sweets. There was a pound note inside the card with love from Aunty Sylvia. Her gift made me burst into tears. Why couldn't someone like her have been my mum?

January brought the coldest winter for a century and I still hadn't been able to get transferred from the farm party. Week-long power cuts meant the cows had to be milked by hand. Big girls like Daisy didn't like cold hands on their tits – a vicious kick from her and you were lying in the shit gulley covered with the stuff.

There was a break from it every second weekend. Work finished at noon on Saturday and after passing a neatness inspection we were given six shillings spending money and allowed to go into the nearby town of Tonypandy until nine that evening. Anyone even a minute late was on jankers for the following week.

On Sunday evenings Skip changed out of his country gent-style clothes to don his Captain's uniform and pre-side over the weekly chapel service. Families from nearby cottages came to swell the congregation and the boys from the home were expected to attend. There was never any bible thumping during the week and with nothing much else happening on Sundays the chapel was as good as any place to be.

Skip had a brother who was also a captain with the Army and at the start of the New Year he joined the staff. He was good on the piano so I thought I'd try to impress him by composing a hymn which could be sung in the chapel. He liked it and for several Sundays it became a favourite everyone joined in with. Whenever Salvation Army bigwigs descended to inspect the home I'd be sent for along with Fred, whose voice was even bigger than mine, to give another impromptu performance. In the polite conversation which followed I plugged away at being unhappy on the farm. 'I'll have a quiet word with Skip,' would be the promise but he refused to be budged.

At the time Skip's promotion to Major came through he was rushed into hospital to have some gallstones removed. While he was away his more relaxed and easy going brother took over. Skip would joke and rough and tumble but even then a part of him still expressed that he was in charge, that he liked being so. With him out of the way grumbling and discontent from the farm work party began to surface. With six months behind me in the home I'd filled out from the skinny stick-kid I'd been. I'd also risen as a natural leader who handed out nicknames to bully boys like Mr Ed who was granted a place at my dining table where I sold him left-over food because he was always hungry.

I still hadn't given up all hope of being transferred off the farm party. I thought if I made myself really useful it still might happen. It was easy persuading a group from the farm party to make their point by absconding. I gave them plenty of time to get away before confiding in the Captain what those stupid boys had done. In the dining room at tea the six empty places were noticeable. The Captain sat looking remote, even hurt. At least his opinion of me had improved. I wasn't guilty of absconding.

I thought I really must be in favour when he asked me later that evening if I wanted to take a ride with him in the big green van, whispering he was on his way to pick up the six runaways being held at a police station at the other side of the valley. Just before we got there he turned serious, stopped laughing at my jokes and said he didn't want me to say a word to the others when they climbed into the back of the van, to show his disapproval. I was with him on that.

The journey back to the home was a sad one for the absconders. They were bedraggled from the rain which had fallen all day and in serious trouble for their recent escapade. I sat next to the Captain, chuffed. The pair of us found plenty to laugh about. The best part was three miles away from the home when he ordered the absconders to get out and made them run the rest of the way in the glare of our headlights. Before going happily to bed, I did mention to the Captain how the coveted job of kitchen assistant would soon be coming vacant.

It was pitch black when the home's fire alarm woke me. I knew the drill and in less than a minute was lining up on the outside forecourt with the rest of the lads. The rain had stopped but it was uncomfortably cold waiting for half an hour before a member of staff made an appearance. Captain Tribble gave a short lecture about inconsiderate individuals and promised the next time any group thought about going walkabout they might find themselves standing out on the yard for the whole night.

As we turned to file back into the house and our beds the Captain called me to follow him into his office. 'You are one of the most deviously unpleasant boys I've ever had the misfortune to come across.' These were the last words I'd expected to hear. He went on, 'Don't think for one moment that your performance yesterday had me fooled. I've been watching you dishing out nicknames and run-

59

ning down other boys. People in glass houses shouldn't throw stones.' Before dismissing me he said that when Skip returned from hospital he would hear the whole story.

The usual Sunday evening routine was changed when we all piled into the van to attend a Salvation Army service in Cardiff. After the hymns and prayers the main speaker began the customary invitation for those who hadn't yet done so to come down to the penitents bench in front of the stage as a sign they wanted to give their life to Jesus. The same thing always used to happen at the House of the Trees chapel and I found it difficult to resist the persuasive arguments which went with the invitation. Who wouldn't want to be saved if they were lost? The fringe benefits sounded very attractive. I wanted Jesus to come into my life but there was a problem which always confused me. I was five feet seven tall. Jesus as a grown man must have been at least six feet. The invitation was as confusing as trying to make a sandwich with the filling on the outside. I wanted to know how Jesus could possibly fit inside me?

Some of the lads from the home began leaving their seats but I was afraid to move. There was an electric tension in the hall as more and more went forward. I would have stayed put if one of the dignitaries on the stage hadn't left the platform and come and taken me by the arm. Immediately tears began streaming down my face. Then I was kneeling down with others beside me giving my life to Christ. On the journey back to the home I felt very strange. As if everything around me was part of a peaceful dream. It lasted for several days before beginning to fade but during that time I was moved to surreptitiously return some money I had stolen from Skip's bedroom and hadn't got round to spending.

One summer's day I was sent with others from the farm party to help a neighbouring farmer with his chores. It was always a bonus to be selected because he never expected to get much work out of us and was content to leave us larking around in his barn all day.

I'd never taken much notice of Mick, a red-haired boy. I'd always thought he was a bit of a wimp but I liked wrestling and was rolling around the straw with him. We carried on through the afternoon and I began to notice how, when our bodies got locked together, Mick would engineer himself underneath me and then stop struggling. Since leaving Eastbourne I hadn't dared even hint I liked having sex with other boys. The body language from Mick and my own growing excitement convinced me it was worth taking a chance.

The opportunity came that evening. Two volunteers from the farm party were needed to stay up overnight to attend one of the sows about to give birth. She conveniently produced a litter by midnight leaving Mick and I to fashion a bed out of straw and old overcoats. The glow from an infra-red lamp warming the new piglets cast enough light for me to see Mick lying down with his back towards me just a few inches away. I only had to reach out and touch him but I was too afraid to make the first move. It had been different at Churchill House: we knew why we had gone to a quiet spot in the woods or an unused room. Other boys had never turned away pretending to be asleep. I could see Mick's tangled mop of red hair and vague memories from way back brought to mind another face with red hair turning towards me. My hand moved fractionally towards Mick, afraid he might turn and say, 'I don't like this.' A few feet away the sound of satisfied grunts and squeals as babies scuffled for an available teat. It took me three hours at least before my fingers brushed the hardness between Mick's legs. Another age before the zip was undone so I could hold him in my hand. He shivered and I felt his fluid in my fingers. He moved, as if asleep, to signal he was tired. I was wide awake. It had been like stealing – the same stealth only far more dangerous.

As a reward for staying up all night I spent the next day on light duties. I had all morning to sweep, dust and polish the chapel but I wasn't concentrating on that. I was reliving what had happened in the night. I'd given Mick that lovely feeling and then he had gone to sleep. If I did the same to myself I could get these thoughts out of my head. At last I gave myself permission and closed the door of the vestry. It felt wrong. On the other side of the wall was where Jesus was prayed and sung to. I overcame my reluctance and in a few moments the only good feeling I knew was wiped away. In its place came something new. A sharp pain sliced a path through my chest. The pain had a name I recognized: Queer.

A few days later the pig shed caught fire. It was evening and someone started spotted the flames from the games room. With the other lads I ran towards the smoke. There were mothers and babies in danger. I got there first. The roof of the pig shed was completely ablaze and the animals were in a state of terror. I could hear their screams. It would be dangerous to enter but I didn't want one of the other lads to be seen to be braver than me. A deep breath and I was inside the thick smoke, then there were others with me, herding the pigs out to safety.

Sheep grazed freely over the mountain slopes next to the farm. They had to be chased off when they got into our fields or they would eat the crops. One afternoon three of us were getting annoyed with a pregnant ewe which kept trotting away and then, at a distance, started chewing again. It was my idea when we caught her to throw her over the cliff at the bottom of the field. It was a thirty-foot sheer drop onto the rocks below. I was curious to see what death looked like as we swung the ewe over the edge to the count of three. She fell, twisting in the air, smashing onto the rocks on her back, but the fall didn't kill her. She tried to get to her feet, her chest heaving in spasms. Blood came from her mouth and nose. We couldn't wait around to watch the end. At any moment someone could spot us and discover what we'd done at the bottom of the field.

The ewe was discovered and somehow Skip put two and two together. Questions were asked and by a process of elimination the three of us stood in front of him to explain ourselves. I could see the contempt in his eyes when I tried to excuse myself by saying I'd only been following along with what the other two culprits were doing.

When the time came for me to leave the House of the Trees I didn't want to go. The only advantage in doing so would be no more cold early-morning showers and the farm. I put up the expected show of being pleased that my time was up but I'd come to see the place as my home. I said goodbye at breakfast time, walking round the room and shaking hands with everyone. I had to fight to hold back my tears. I couldn't let anyone know how I felt. I was sixteen and the hardest in the home. Sitting next to Skip as he drove me in the van to the station I thought how I was always being driven away from where I wanted to be.

CHAPTER 10

I WAS ON MY WAY BACK TO LIVE NEAR THE VILLAGE IN BARKINGSIDE where Aunty Sylvia had offered me a temporary home. I was going to apply to join the Royal Navy but the process of selection would take several weeks. Her son Stephen made an attempt to welcome me, but I could sense he wasn't pleased: he remembered too well the things I'd stolen from him years before. Now at college and into the Who and Bob Dylan, his mum said he was going through a difficult phase. Spurred on by her he made a token gesture of friendship by inviting me to visit Carnaby Street with him. As soon as we got there he forgot about me. I spent the day following him round shop after shop as he searched for the right coloured pair of flared trousers.

I soon learnt the Navy was cautious about recruiting convicted thieves. They told me to keep out of trouble for a year and try again. Aunty Sylvia was disappointed and advised me to look for a job. My first enquiry resulted in me working as a messenger boy for an advertising film company in London's West End.

The five pounds a week wages barely covered living expenses but I was able to double my income by claiming for non-existent taxi fares. It was much quicker delivering on foot anyway and I loved dodging through thick crowds on the hectic streets, but at weekends the loneliness returned. I had money in my pocket and nobody to share it with.

Since the West End was the only area I was familiar with, I returned there on Saturdays. At first I spent the day in picture houses but one day I spotted some publicity photos outside a theatre in St Martin's Lane. The show was *Oliver* but it was the young boys in the pictures that attracted me inside. When the show was over I hung around the stage door hoping to catch sight of the juvenile actors. I wanted to be close to them. I wanted to hold the boy who played Oliver and sang 'Where is Love', tell him I, too, was lonely. They came out together in a group and I followed them to a nearby amusement arcade but I didn't go in. I watched from the other side of the street thinking what I was feeling was wrong. Nobody would understand. But for months my Saturdays never varied: I watched the matinee and evening performance of *Oliver* every week.

Within a few weeks I'd tested Aunty Sylvia's patience to the limit. She wasn't entirely happy with me working in the West End and a phone call from a strange man asking for me made matters worse. I'd met him on my way to deliver a can of film and had stopped to stroke his Alsatian dog. The man was so friendly I agreed to go to his flat round the corner to meet his other dog and I was too embarrassed to refuse when he asked if he could pull down my trousers.

Aunty's pride and joy was the Triumph Herald she'd bought after passing her driving test. She cleaned and polished it every week and kept it in a row of garages a few streets away. One Sunday afternoon I stole the ignition keys from her handbag. My only experience of driving was in a tractor and as a result Aunty's car received an ugly gash from one end of the coachwork to the other. When gently questioned about the damage I denied all knowledge. She didn't press me but I was sure that she didn't believe me.

Aunty must have spoken to my probation officer who suggested I move into a youth hostel in Putney. I didn't blame Aunty for having had enough of me and the hostel had the bonus of sharing a room with a boy I found fascinating. He was like a girl. The elegant way he moved reminded me of the young footballer who had confused me so much at school. Ian worked as a trainee hairdresser and after weeks of persuasion allowed me to jump into his bed one night. He kept insisting he was only interested in older men but for thirty shillings saved from my taxi fiddle at work he made an exception. Afterwards I thought it was an expensive price for ten minutes pleasure.

I wanted to be famous, so I bought a copy of *The Stage* and studied the ads in the back. One caught my attention: 'David Keller, singing coach, has vacancies. Engagements found for all suitable students.' It cost two pounds a lesson but I was sure that I'd only need a few to make my stage début. For a month I worked on my rendition of 'Hello Dolly' and refining the hand movements which my teacher called 'presentation'. I thought I was ready. *The Stage* carried an ad inviting singers to audition for a new Lionel Bart musical at the Shaftesbury Theatre. It was to be called *Twang* and was based on the story of Robin Hood. A lot of people were already backstage when I arrived, some stood alone practising their scales or warming up their voices, others who seemed to know each other milled around chatting. Nobody took any notice of me, but I wasn't concerned.

I was full of confidence when it came to my audition. I walked on to the vast West End stage and handed the sheet music for 'Hello Dolly' to the man at the piano. The house lights were down but halfway up the auditorium I could make out a small group of people lit by the glow of a single light bulb. I gave my name, as instructed, listened to the familiar bars of the song's introduction, then launched into my number. I gave it everything but my voice didn't seem to travel much further than the orchestra pit. I tried to increase volume but the hand movements I'd been taught got mixed up leaving me waving at the wrong times. I'm not sure who finished first, the pianist or me. I was naive enough to believe the voice from the stalls which called out: 'Thank you. We'll be in touch'.

In the summer of 1965 I travelled back to Eastbourne to visit the boys and staff at Churchill House. I'd put off the visit until I could return in splendour. I'd always remembered the deep impression made on me when I lived in the home when another old boy used to visit. Everybody used to comment on his beautiful brown suit and matching shoes. Since then I'd had it fixed in my mind that clothes were the measure of your success. I'd stolen some money from a briefcase left lying about at work and had spent the twenty-five pounds on a complete new wardrobe.

I was shocked to discover that Churchill House had been bulldozed to the ground and the home had been relocated to two cottages at the bottom of the old football field. Mr Brown had moved on and in the eighteen months I'd been away so many new faces had taken up residence I didn't feel I had any connection with the place. By coincidence, the boy I'd been caught naked in the sick bay with chose to visit the same weekend so my journey back to Eastbourne wasn't entirely wasted.

I decided on impulse to write to Barnardo's asking if they could put me back in touch with my mother. The following week a letter arrived. There were the usual apologies for being my mum plus a date when she would be coming to London for the day. We met on a Saturday morning but I barely recognized the woman who walked past the ticket barrier at Euston station and said, 'Hello, John.' In the eight years since I'd last seen her, I'd forgotten what she looked like. I realized that I didn't like the way she spoke. As a nine-year-old I'd been ignorant of accents, but I now disliked my mother's Black Country twang. Politely playing host, I asked what she would like to do. Buckingham Palace was first on her list. We stood together peering through the railings which separated us from the royal residence. My mother seemed as excited as a child, thinking the Queen might appear at any moment. I didn't tell her the flag on top of the building wasn't flying so the Queen was not at home.

As we were about to leave for the Tower, my mother began talking to a woman she obviously knew. Listening in, it became apparent that my mother had travelled to London with a group of friends. My mother introduced me to her friend as 'the person I was telling you about'. I don't remember what we did for the rest of the day or how we said goodbye. The only thing I knew was that my mum couldn't acknowledge me as her son.

The last time we met I'd just turned eighteen. I caught a train to Birmingham while she travelled down to our rendezvous from her home in Stafford. She linked her arm through mine as we window-shopped in the city centre. I'd rarely felt so embarrassed. I imagined people were looking at this curious couple, speculating on what possible relationship could exist between us. Most, I assumed, would think this young black man and middle-aged woman were lovers. Sitting inside a café I gave my mother the pottery vase I'd wrapped as a present. She gave a squeal of delight and began hurriedly unwrapping my gift. At that moment a familiar flood of resentment swept over me: the speed at which she opened her present convinced me she was greedy but she had nothing to give to me.

It had never occurred to me I might have half-brothers and sisters so it was quite a surprise when my mother produced from her handbag photographs of her other children. I looked at the images but like my mother the faces were strangers to me. I learnt that my mother was married with a young family when she met my father. They had only known each other six weeks before he returned to Nigeria. Discovering she was pregnant she confessed to her husband who said he would forgive her on one condition. If the baby she was carrying was born black she would have to put it in a Home. If it turned out white, it would be smuggled into the family as if it was his own. I looked across the café table at my mother. Her hair was naturally blonde. She had blue eyes and I could see how as a young girl she must have been quite beautiful.

I asked why she had stopped writing to me at the children's home. I might have guessed. When Mr Jolliffe the superintendent had invited her to lunch he had advised her to break off contact. He'd convinced her it was for the best because, in his opinion, I'd become disturbed since first meeting her. I told her how wrong he had been, how for the past couple of years I'd thought she might have been offended because on the envelope of my last letter from Shackleford House I'd written SWALK, 'Sealed With A Loving Kiss'. There wasn't much more I wanted to say to her so I suggested we spend the afternoon at the cinema watching *A Hard Day's Night*. Afterwards we walked back to the railway station. On the way I was trying to calculate whether my mother loved me enough to pay for my train fare back to London. I was embarrassed to tell her I only had a few coppers in my pocket. At the booking office I politely let her stand in front of me and was relieved as she bought my ticket. My train was the first to leave and before it pulled away my mother reminded me how she always said a special prayer for me before going to bed. I said I would write to her but I knew that I wouldn't. It was much too late for her to ever really be my mum.

I'd been delivering cans of film for eight months when I saw an advertisement in *The Stage* for a trainee lighting assistant at the Mermaid theatre in Puddle Dock. Although there were scores of applicants, the job was offered to me. But there was a problem: the hostel where I lived closed its doors at ten-thirty so I would have to find somewhere else to live if I wanted to work at the Mermaid.

I took my problem to Edwin who lived in a flat overlooking Chelsea Barracks. Edwin – tall, overweight and in his early thirties – had been introduced to me by Maurice from the film company's art department. Edwin was openly gay and I was aware he found me attractive (even though I couldn't understand why). I explained how much I wanted the job at the Mermaid and he said I could move into his spare bedroom if I wanted. I wanted to believe Edwin was simply helping me out so I pretended not to mind when he pressed his flabby body close to mine in the narrow single bed.

Starting work at the Mermaid, I told people my name was Oliver, John felt too common. The show in production was a comedy called *Let's Get a Divorce*, starring Fenella Fielding. My first responsibility was backstage operating a tape machine which produced the various sound effects. Carefully following the marked script, I had to get the telephone on stage to ring or the door to rap on cue. When the time came for the audience to applaud I imagined their appreciation was for me, even taking an unseen bow. When Miss Fielding acknowledged me in a corridor one day, I thought I was but a short step from being famous myself.

I didn't last long at Edwin's flat. He returned unexpectedly from a holiday in Greece to find I'd invited two of the older boys from the Eastbourne children's home to stay. He gave me a week to find another room and I found one in King's Cross. Money wasn't a problem: soon after starting work at the Mermaid I began nipping into offices and dressing rooms helping myself to unguarded cash. If I saw twenty pounds in a drawer I'd take ten, reasoning that people were like me, always losing things, and would assume they had spent or mislaid the cash. Six weeks later, I was caught, having stolen something from almost every person backstage.

The Magistrate remanded me in custody for a week while the police made further enquiries into the theft of a pair of shoes from the hostel where I'd previously lived. Locked up in a cell at Ashford Remand Centre I bitterly regretted the impulse to take the shoes – they hadn't even fitted me anyway.

The other two lads in the cell were old hands at Ashford and explained how the place was the same as adult prisons, but stricter. I didn't feel uncomfortable in this environment, but was concerned about my room and few belongings at King's Cross. On the first day, I was interviewed by the governor and the priest. The doctor, also present, sat behind her desk and asked if I had any problems. Grateful to find someone interested in me I said yes, going on to outline the guilt I was experiencing at being homosexual. She interrupted me to ask if I'd made any advances towards my cell-mates. Later that day a prison officer came to the cell and instructed the two lads to get their kit packed and I spent the rest of the week on my own. At the magistrates' court I apologized for the trouble I'd caused and was fined ten pounds.

It was good to be free and out on the street in the warm sunshine. I had reason to be glad it was summer because I soon discovered I no longer had a roof over my head. My key still fitted the lock to my bedsit, but someone else's possessions were scattered around the room: the landlord had re-let. I spent the first night on a bench in St James' Park. The next day I returned to the Mermaid and asked for

71

the week's wages I'd missed. The manager was taken aback at my cheek, but paid me all the same. I found a bed in a Streatham hostel, but hated it there. The rent used up what money I had left and it was a rule at the house you were out by nine and not allowed back in before five in the afternoon.

Hot, hungry and very lonely, I paid a visit one morning to Edwin's flat. I knew he would be out at work and it would be easy to break in, but there was nothing of any value to steal. I contented myself with a camera and portable typewriter. The owner of a second-hand shop agreed a price of ten pounds and was just about to hand me the money when two burly men in suits stepped out from a room behind the counter. I made a dash for the door but it was too late. One of the policemen caught hold of my arm, flung me hard on the floor, then sat with all his weight on my chest. I was wearing a silver crucifix on a chain round my neck which infuriated my captor. Sitting in my face he told me how much he despised Black Nigger Catholics.

I spent the rest of the summer on remand. In October, the Judge sentenced me to three months at a detention centre. It was supposed to be a short, sharp, shock but, on settling in, I enjoyed being there. The regime placed a lot of emphasis on sporting achievement and with my natural ability as a runner I was able to avoid punishment for lack of effort. Every weekend, the hundred or so inmates were timed over a circuit in the gym. A supposedly unbeatable record for the course had stood for years so when I bettered it there was a lot of praise and congratulations. One of the PT instructors was impressed and suggested I join an athletics club when my three months were up.

I didn't know where I was going to live, but I'd had enough of London. The House of the Trees had been the last place where I had felt secure and Cardiff was just a few miles away. The three months at Goudhurst detention centre passed in a flash and one sunny day in January I headed back to Wales carrying an introductory letter and the address of the probation department in Cardiff.

As soon as I arrived I knew I would like my new home. The city centre was busy with people shopping for sale bargains but unlike London there were smiles on their faces and they had time for friends to stop and chat. One of the first things I noticed were young men with light brown skin like mine. Quite a few nodded in my direction and said hello.

The probation department was expecting me and I was given directions to a house where digs had been arranged, one of a long line of terraced dwellings in Swan Street. It was a tight squeeze inside with the landlady, her husband, two sons and three other lodgers all recently released from one or another of Her Majesty's establishments. A week after I moved in there was a knock on the front door. A boy of about fourteen in school uniform asked if Dennis, the landlady's youngest son, was coming out to play. I said he wasn't in and slowly closed the door. I felt like I'd been punched hard in the stomach. I told myself I'd just seen the most beautiful boy in the world. His face was thin but his lips seemed huge. He had a wide nose and slightly freckled skin. Most striking of all were his grey-blue eyes fringed with lashes as long as a girl's. I'd only had a few seconds to look at him but I felt for certain I had fallen in love.

Over the next few days I casually prised snippets of information from Dennis about his friend. His name was Patrick, he lived round the corner and they had been friends for ages. Dennis shared a room with me and two of the other lodgers who spent most evenings in the pub. One night while they were out drinking, in the darkened bedroom I engineered the conversation towards Patrick. I asked if they were close friends. Dennis surprised me by confessing he didn't really like Patrick very much. I sensed his embarrassment when I asked him what he meant. I knew Dennis didn't want to say more but when I pressed him he blurted out, 'I think he's a homo.' A great hope welled up in me as Dennis's information sunk home. At last I'd found someone to love. Now the confession had been made I swooped for further confirmation. Dennis thought Patrick was a homo because he sometimes wanted to do 'funny things'. I didn't need to know any more, I just needed to get a lot closer to Patrick.

A week later I had to leave Swan Street having stolen a pound note from the pocket of a sleeping lodger and been found out. The probation officer found new lodgings for me a few streets away with a skinny, hatchet-faced woman called Dot and seven other lodgers from different parts of the country who were all on government training courses. Dot let me know that she didn't usually take in unemployed people and that she'd been concerned how her other lodgers would react to a 'coloured boy'. She said she had made an exception in my case because I spoke so nicely and I was sure to find a job. I didn't try too hard. The next day I was snooping around one of the shared bedrooms and found a locked suitcase. I opened it with a pin and found seventy pounds. It was the most money I'd ever had, enough to buy a second-hand Vespa as well as a pair of running shoes.

Cardiff had two running clubs, Roath and Birchgrove Harriers. I signed up with the latter and was made very welcome. After a few training sessions, older and more experienced athletes and coaches all predicted great things from me. At first I kept to my training schedule but all I could think of was getting away from the stadium as early as possible. It was spring and the evenings were warm. If I was lucky I might see Patrick playing in the street or on the fruit machine in the local café. I started work as a lens grinder in a factory producing slide projectors but my mind was only half on the job. I spent most of the day creating romantic fantasies involving Patrick and me. Any day which passed without seeing him felt like a waste.

I moved on from Dot's house after being arrested for breaking open one of the electricity meters. I got away with two shillings but left my fingerprints behind. My probation officer composed a report for the magistrates which detailed what a deceitful little shit I was and the local paper carried a brief item giving my name and the offence. I was worried what the members of Birchgrove Harriers might think so I stayed away and gave up training. I moved into a small bedsit in Emerald Street, which suited me as it was a few yards closer to Patrick's house. It was also nearer Rashid's café where most of the local boys spent the evenings playing the flipper machines. I called in there every evening to buy chips and curry sauce. Patrick was often there but I was still too shy to even say hello.

Soon I established myself as a regular at the café. Instead of just serving me, Rashid encouraged me to sit and talk with him. He was a lonely man and I had the impression I was taking on the role of surrogate son. He laughed out loud one evening when I explained how deeply I'd offended the muslim landlady at my latest address. She had screamed at me and smashed defiled plates after discovering a tin of beans and pork sausages in her kitchen waste-bin. Rashid told me not to worry and said if I liked I could move into one of the empty rooms above his café. I jumped at the chance – everything was working out perfectly. I would be living in the place Patrick spent much of his free time. Even better, I knew that he and Dennis had fallen out.

One evening while Rashid and I were tucking into a beef curry somebody climbed through the back kitchen window and stole the week's takings from a drawer. When Rashid discovered the theft his dark brown wizened face went pale with shock. He often gambled on the horses and I knew he was quite heavily in debt. The police were called in but it was clear they weren't convinced a crime had been committed. One confided to me his opinion that the money had been lost in the bookies'. About eleven that evening, one of the regular visitors to the café whispered the name of the culprit in Rashid's ear. Rashid passed the information on to me and because I liked him so much that it felt as if I, too, had been robbed I decided to do something about it. The thief's name was Kenny Fisher who lived round the corner in Swan Street. Everybody knew the Fishers. You didn't just knock on their door and ask please could we have our money back. Mrs Fisher, at seventeen stone, was the Ma Baker of the local community and Kenny was her oldest son. Just as intimidating was the reputation of her equally massive and violent brothers.

The policemen on duty that night at the station listened to my suspicions and left en masse to call on the Fishers. I followed and stood at a discreet distance, opposite the Fishers' house. 'Open the door, Joan,' a policeman called through the letterbox after knocking several times. 'It's the police. We want a few words with Kenny.'

'Fuck off you pig bastards!' screamed back Mrs Fisher from an open upstairs window.

Curtains in the street started twitching. A few people ventured out and watched curiously from their doorsteps.

'If you don't open up, this door is coming down,' a police sergeant shouted back. There was a long silence, then the front door opened. Kenny Fisher walked out and climbed meekly into the back of the police transit van. As it pulled away Mrs Fisher stood at the window screaming further threats. To the great satisfaction of the locals, some weeks

76

later Kenny Fisher was sent to a detention centre for three months.

I eventually made friends with Patrick after giving him money to play on the café's machines. From then on he began calling for me to go swimming with him or for a ride on my scooter. When he asked me for the scooter, I gave it to him willingly. I was a bit hurt to discover he didn't want it for himself but for his older sister's boyfriend. Patrick sang in the choir at the local Catholic church so I began attending and started taking weekly instruction to become a Catholic myself. Although I was four years older, Patrick soon established himself as the boss. Whatever he wanted, he got: I even liked the way he ordered me around. I didn't want to lose him so I never let on that I found him sexually attractive. I was always very aware that Patrick was still only a child.

I knew something had gone wrong when I saw Patrick playing football in the street with his former friend Dennis. I said hello, but they both ignored me. The next time I saw Patrick he was feeding coins into a fruit machine. I pleaded with him to tell me what I'd done wrong but he wouldn't speak and acted as if I didn't exist. When he stopped coming to the café I thought I'd lost him for good.

Helen, a dark-haired lumpy woman, was one of the café's regulars. Always dressed in a shapeless blue anorak and thick spectacles, I'd only known her for a few weeks when she invited me to her house for Sunday dinner and suggested that I might like to live there as one of the family. Her husband was enthusiastic. Her three young daughters said they liked the idea of having a big brother. The one snag was that I had to share a bedroom with Helen's fourteen-year-old son. She asked if I'd mind, but I didn't.

Rashid's face fell when I told him I was moving. I knew I

would miss him but I was caught up with the idea of acquiring a ready-made family. My enthusiasm only lasted for a few weeks. On Fridays I'd been giving Helen my wages on the understanding she would start a savings account for me, but whenever I asked for money she never seemed to have it.

After a while I also realized that Helen was interested in me sexually. One night we sat up till the early hours of the morning and it all came out. I explained that I was very much in love with Patrick, which made her cry. I knew then that yet again I'd have to find somewhere new to live.

I moved back to Swan Street where Big Joan Fisher made room for me. She had never expressed any anger at the part I'd played in her son's arrest and always stopped to chat when I saw her out at the shops in Clifton Street. I was a bit concerned about Kenny who was due for release from the detention centre, but Joan assured me it was all in the past. What made up for this worry was that I was living near Patrick again. He still wouldn't acknowledge me but at least he was close.

Joan's husband was a small tubby man who ran a decorating business. He'd been to prison, as had all the other lodgers in the house. During the evenings and at weekends there were constant visitors, mostly policemen. Joan made them cups of tea then settled in her big armchair to regale them with gossip about her neighbours' wrongdoings. It might be that someone was suspected of working while claiming national assistance or receiving stolen goods. She seemed to know so much about other people I wondered how much she was making up. What surprised me was the openness of Joan's grassing and that the ex-cons in the house also contributed snippets of information.

One Saturday afternoon I got into an argument with one of the Clifton Street lads. There was a scuffle and a lucky punch from me landed my opponent flat on his back. As I walked away I heard him threatening he'd be back with his friends. I remembered how Patrick had once spoken with admiration for a friend of his who had faced up to a gang out to get him. I thought if he heard how I'd done the same he might start talking to me again. That evening, I issued a challenge. The Clifton Street lads were playing on the café machines. I opened the door and shouted, 'You bunch of wankers. If you want to take this afternoon any further see me at two o'clock tomorrow.' The next day, about thirty youths and a handful of girls were waiting.

It was too near the police station to battle it out on Clifton Street so a noisy procession followed me to a deserted alley behind the garage where I'd bought my scooter. Ginger Smith led the attack. Head down he rushed in like a charging bull. I swung my fist in the general direction of his face and felt it connect with a dull crunch. He staggered back under the force of the blow, an avalanche of blood pouring from his broken nose. The crowd moved back unnerved by my early success. They were reluctant to meet the same fate. I could sense their fear. I felt capable of defeating them all. I wanted them to scatter and run so I picked up an empty milk bottle, smashed the bottom of it against the wall behind me and moved threateningly towards the enemy. 'Come on you shit coward bastards,' I taunted, 'Who's next?' They moved back a step as if one.

'Cunts the lot of you. Come and get some stitches in your ugly gobs.' They hadn't bargained for this. Didn't want to know.

'Fight me? You bunch of wankers,' I sneered. 'You couldn't beat a fucking egg.' I felt capable of taking on the whole world with one hand tied behind my back so when one plaintive voice called out from the crowd 'Fight fair.' I contemptuously threw my weapon aside. They came at me all at once but in the crush no one could land an effective punch or kick. Then Joan Fisher's husband and a posse of lodgers turned up in a van. The mob fled, and I went back to Swan Street feeling like a king.

Sure enough, news of the fight spread and Patrick started speaking to me again. I was even invited to his house. Sitting next to him on the couch in the neat front parlour I knew what it was to feel perfectly content. But trouble was brewing at the Fishers'.

A few days previously one of the lodgers had been thrown out. Tom, a grey unhealthy-looking man, worked at the same factory as me and in a tea break we talked about recent events. He was still smarting from his abrupt eviction and had little good to say about the Fishers. 'That twerp of a husband's a poof,' he concluded. Encouraged by this disclosure, I mentioned how a boy from the café had told me that Joan's husband had once tried to touch him up. Later, in an attempt to get back in Joan's good books, Tom told her I'd been spreading rumours that her husband was a poof. Totally unaware, I returned home from Patrick's house to find Tom sitting in his usual chair in the kitchen with a sly smile on his face as Joan screamed and swore and told me to get out of her house.

Patrick's mum and dad said I could spend the night at their house. I didn't explain why I'd been thrown out and living round the corner from the Fishers they didn't really want to know. I'd always seen Patrick's parents as a cut above their neighbours and it felt like an honour to be invited to stay. I wanted them to approve of me, to say I could stay forever. Patrick was showing me pictures from the family photograph album when there was a loud knock on the front door. Joan had sent one of the lodgers to summon me back to the house. I followed him round and walked into Joan's kitchen which felt like a courtroom. The judge was one of her big dangerous brothers who sat sprawled in an armchair eating chips from a newspaper. The boy from the café who had told me about Joan's husband touching him up was standing nervously in the corner. I knew the reason he couldn't look was that he was going to lie and deny that he'd ever said what I repeated to the lodger. Joan said he could go. The huge brother took this as his cue to screw up his fish and chip paper which he then used to wipe his greasy mutton-chop moustache. Satisfied with his brush up, he lumbered lazily from his chair towards me. I knew the best thing to do was cover up but he was still very efficient with his fists.

I'm not sure whether I got out of the house under my own steam or was kicked down the hall and out onto the street. I did hear Joan shouting, though. 'That will teach you to tell lies about my husband!' Patrick's parents were shocked at seeing how bruised and bloodied I was. I found it impossible not to cry when Patrick rushed me into the back kitchen and began tenderly cleaning my wounds with cotton wool. Afraid the Fishers might return, Patrick's parents drove me to a relative's house a few miles away. I contented myself with Patrick's promise to meet me after mass the following day.

I felt as if the Fishers had robbed me of everything. The tiny hope that I might be able to live at Patrick's house had been destroyed and there was nothing left worth living for. After mass, I walked into the centre of Cardiff to find a chemist's. I bought five hundred aspirin and made my way to the shed that Patrick had turned into a den decorated with naked girlie pin-ups. I washed down a couple of handfuls of pills with lemonade and sat and waited. I thought about what I'd done and started to feel scared, no longer quite so sure I wanted to die. What if it was Patrick who found me dead? If I died, I'd never see him again. Feeling a bit wobbly, I walked in a sort of dream to the priory at St Peter's. The silver-haired priest who had been giving me weekly instruction opened the door. 'Oh you silly child!' he cried out, when I told him what I'd done, then rushed to call a taxi to take me to hospital.

The doctor sent the nurse for warm salt water and a bucket. He said he hoped the mixture made me sick because I wouldn't enjoy having my stomach pumped. It might teach me a lesson, though. As he and the nurse encouraged me to stick my fingers down my throat, I could sense their irritation. I'd expected drama and fuss but there were no concerned faces crowding the small cubicle anxious to know what made me feel desperate enough to try killing myself. I felt a little better when I learnt I would be admitted for twenty-four hours. I was sure I would get some attention when I got to the ward.

The news soon reached Patrick's house and his grandmother was my first visitor. She told me the door to her house would always be open if ever I felt like visiting. I thanked her but as Patrick didn't live there I doubted I would take her up on the offer. He came in the afternoon and told me I was a fool which, coming from him, I knew must be true. A social worker finally sat by my bed and listened to my reasons for swallowing so many aspirin. She said little but at least helped solve my accommodation problem by telephoning the YMCA.

My new home had many advantages. I had my own small room and breakfast and an evening meal were served downstairs. I was living at least a mile away from Patrick so I intended to get him out of my mind, find a new job and work on my running. Birchgrove Harriers were pleased to see me back. I assured them that this time I was serious and would train every day. Not wishing to return to the factory where Joan Fisher's lodger still worked, I applied for a job as a pharmacy porter at the local hospital. The administrator who interviewed me wore a small silver cross in his lapel. I felt sure he offered me the job because I explained why I'd so recently been a patient.

My work in the hospital delivering drugs to the wards gave me a feeling of responsibility: I was one of a team looking after the sick. When the crash call alarm was sounded I wanted more than anything to race alongside the doctors hurrying to save a patient who had gone into a cardiac arrest. When I'd been at the hospital for about three months, I stole an infra-red lamp from the physiotherapy department. It was one of many so I thought it wouldn't be missed. Various members of Birchgrove Harriers often remarked how useful an infra-red lamp would be and I could see their grateful faces when I brought it into the club. Somehow the police got to hear of my generosity and once again I was hauled before the magistrates. The punishment was a ten-pound fine and, of course, I was sacked.

I moved back to the Clifton Street area of Cardiff on my twentieth birthday having done a moonlight flit from the YMCA because I was several weeks behind with my rent. I took a room in Railway Street, near the Bomb and Dagger club where Shirley Bassey began her singing career. I hadn't been there long before Patrick called. He'd run away from home. My feelings for him still hadn't diminished and I was overjoyed. He said his mum and dad were too bossy and he was never going back but I could hardly believe he was going to stay for even one night, let alone forever.

There was little furniture in my room so we had to squeeze together, spoon-shaped, in the narrow single bed. I was afraid Patrick could hear my heart pounding. I was terrified. Patrick looked over his shoulder and said matter of factly, 'Let's have it off.' For two years I'd wanted nothing else, but I thought I'd imagined what I'd heard. He spoke again: 'You fool.' I couldn't move and a few minutes later I knew he was asleep. The next morning he said he was going home.

CHAPTER 11

ONE OF THE REGULAR CUSTOMERS IN THE ALL-NIGHT CAFÉ where I now worked had his own café in the red-light district of the town. He had to go home to Turkey urgently and said I could take over the tenancy for forty pounds. I soon found out why it was so cheap. The café was sandwiched in the middle of a row of crumbling buildings shored up by thick wooden beams and obviously due for demolition. I didn't raise the full amount required but as it was so late in the day he introduced me to the owner and handed over the keys. The café had once been painted blue, but when was anybody's guess. Inside were a few ancient wooden tables and chairs, a football game and a juke box. The small, greasy kitchen boasted a filthy gas oven and little else. Even egg, sausage and chips would have been a problem in that kitchen. I needn't have worried: the working girl customers were satisfied with tea or coffee and somewhere warm to wait between punters.

Jackie was older than most of the girls and covered her face with make-up to disguise the fact. She reminded me of a thin tired clown and I thought it funny when she offered to keep me. Most of the girls apparently had a man to whom they gave part of their earnings. I didn't conceal from Jackie that I was more interested in the boys who came in to play on the football machine but she started giving me money anyway. When she wasn't with a punter she helped out in the kitchen.

I liked this new world. I stopped training with Birchgrove Harriers and began discovering clubs and drugs. Around the corner from the café on the main road was a gay pub where I started going every evening. I always checked that nobody I knew saw me enter. The Blue Anchor was a scruffy, seedy place with bare wooden floors. I always hoped to meet someone young there, but the average age of the customers was at least forty.

Sitting in one of Cardiff's trendiest cafés, I took my first illegal drug. I was with Keith, a boy with dark good looks who maintained he was straight and had wandered into the Blue Anchor by mistake. He passed a capsule across the table to me and said it was a Green and White. I could tell he meant it as a gift and assumed that, because I was a couple of years older, I knew about such things so I swallowed it and waited. Thirty minutes later I thought I was in heaven. Everything around me sparkled and shone, the music on the juke box sounded like nothing I'd ever heard before, and, most amazing of all, feelings of a warmth and a love I'd never realized existed filled my whole body. I sat with Keith for hours perfectly content and said to myself that if I died tomorrow it wouldn't matter because I know what it's like to be happy. Still feeling on top of the world, I got back to the café and promised Jackie I would go home with her that night. We went to bed together but it meant as much to me as, say, doing the washing up. With Jackie's guidance I performed the obligatory fuck, my only difficulty being to muffle the laughter her screams of passion provoked.

Keith and I decided on a weekend in London. We had an unspoken understanding that our trip would involve making money on the Piccadilly rent scene. Jackie said she

85

would mind the café so, one Friday afternoon, Keith and I made a tour of various car parks looking for an easy vehicle to steal. Fifty miles down the motorway in an old Hillman Hunter with a police car behind us, the engine began throwing out thick black smoke. We both panicked and I pulled onto the hard shoulder, jumped out of the car and shouted at Keith to follow me as I took off across the fields. Two coppers in uniform soon gave up chasing us through the mud and after a mile or so we decided to lie low until dark.

Neither of us was sure of our exact location but we thought we were safe when we found a van in a country lane with the keys conveniently left in the ignition. When we eventually found our bearings, we were just a couple of miles outside Cardiff. A police patrol car flashed its lights at us because the headlights of the van were on full beam. I'd already tried, unsuccessfully to dim them. The police car did a swift U-turn and I could see in the van's mirror they were coming up behind us fast so once again we jumped out and took to the fields. Keith and I got separated in the darkness but we met up again an hour later in the police cells. Apparently Keith had been caught almost immediately. It took another hour for the police to catch up with me and I had bites on my leg from the dog which finally ran me to ground.

Jackie bailed me out from the police station and I went back to the café. I was worried. The last time I'd appeared in front of the magistrate he had warned I was in danger of being sent to prison but I'd taken out some insurance against such an eventuality. It was time to call on Sergeant Jackson. I'd first met him at Fat Joan Fisher's house. He was working in the vice squad at the time and in between Joan's latest stories he entertained us with his more lurid cases. Some time later he took me to one side and confessed he needed some help. Apparently he'd been trans-ferred to the drug squad but wasn't having much luck making arrests. What he wanted me to do was find a customer for some purple hearts he would supply, then arrest him as I handed the pills over. I would be allowed to escape. This all went according to plan and the unsuspecting victim went on to supply the sergeant with valuable information.

I went before the magistrate charged with two offences of taking a vehicle without consent confident that the sergeant would keep his promise to have a quiet word behind the scenes. I sensed the magistrate wasn't too happy but he sent Keith to Crown Court with a view to borstal training while only giving me a three-month suspended sentence. The sergeant had let it be known that I was more useful to the police at liberty than locked away. I congratulated myself on having friends in the right places, but two months later I was back in the same court facing a charge of stealing ten pounds. I'd picked up a very effeminate young guy in the Blue Anchor one afternoon and had taken him to a quiet spot in a nearby park. As soon as he'd taken his trousers off, I grabbed them and ran away. The police called at the café the next day but with the suspended sentence hanging over me I denied any involvement. I changed my mind when the officer questioning me explained how embarrassing it could be if the local paper got to print the details of the offence. If I confessed, the seedier side of the event would be forgotten. I had little choice – I was beyond help from the sergeant and I was on my way to prison for three months at least.

The prison wasn't far from Clifton Street. I had passed the grim grey walls each time I walked into town. From the pavement outside you could only see the prison's roof and the line of small barred windows immediately underneath. On warm summer nights I had heard the distant shouts of prisoners as they called to each other, never thinking that one day I would join them.

At twenty I wasn't old enough to be classified as an adult prisoner so after being fingerprinted and asked my personal details I was taken to a small complex separate from the main prison which housed young prisoners waiting on remand and a dozen or so others who, like me, were serving sentences. I was locked into a cell on the top landing. Disappointingly, the window faced away from Clifton Street. When the door was opened to slop out, the first person I saw was someone I knew. He had turned up at the café late one night with nowhere to stay. He was good looking in just the way I liked best: black hair, blue eyes and soft, unshaven skin. We slept together on a mattress in the kitchen and although we wanked each other off, in the morning we pretended nothing had happened. He recognized me as I walked towards him on the landing. He started to smile but then he saw my look of embarrassment and disgust. The last thing I wanted in this place was to be suspected as a queer.

I had six months to serve. With remission for good behaviour my release date fell on New Year's Day which seemed a very long way off. I wondered what Patrick would think when he learnt where I was. I adjusted easily to the prison routine which didn't seem much different to the routine in children's homes. Life there was made even easier when I was given the prized position of gym orderly. The director of Cardiff's youth department was aware of the talent I had shown at the running club and wanted me fully fit and ready for active competition when I left in four months' time. At ten o'clock each evening I would hear through the steel cell door the night watchman's shuffling slippers as he paused to switch off my light before moving on to the next cell and, in the distance, the jovial voices of the late-shift staff going home. Car doors slammed and engines were started. In the quiet of midnight I felt the comforting presence of my childhood's Father God. He hadn't changed – he was the same Father God I could speak to and hear in words which needed no language. The Father I had known before ghosts and nightmares had folded their wings in my mind.

The four months passed more quickly than I imagined. Waiting to meet me outside the prison's main gate was the secretary of the YMCA who had come to say that the past was done with and I could come back to the hostel. With every intention of pursuing my athletic career, for a month I trained regularly. My coach became very excited as my times improved and predicted I would be the first Welshman to break four minutes for the mile. It was the cross-country season. I hated the cold but held my own in races through the sticky mud. People watching me run always said I looked so relaxed. What could I do if I really tried? But my style of running was in part self-imposed, specially designed to conceal any sign of distress or strain from spectators who I feared would otherwise perceive my weakness.

I stopped going to the club after spending an evening at the Blue Anchor. I hadn't meant to stay long but I met a boy my own age called Ivor. His dark hair and soft face guaranteed my interest and as the only two young people in the place we talked while feeding the jukebox. When the pub called time we walked back to the YMCA on my suggestion that we play a few games of snooker, but what happened next took me completely by surprise. After a couple of games, we left the basement room to go upstairs to mine. As I closed the door and was about to switch on the light, Ivor's arms gently pulled me close to his body. He put his lips to mine and suddenly I knew what people saw in snogging! When Patrick had started collecting pictures of naked girls he had asked me how you kissed one properly but I couldn't tell him. Most of my knowledge came from seeing it done in films. Sometimes, when I held a boy's cock in my hand, I'd also wanted to kiss him but I'd never dared do it simply because I didn't think people ever really did it. From my 'Rubber Lips' days at school I thought my lips were ugly but being kissed and kissing Ivor I was beautiful.

It was the Easter bank holiday and the pubs in town were full. I went first into the Cockney Pride and was about to cross the road to the Blue Anchor when Patrick walked in with two of the Clifton Street boys. In the six months since I'd last seen him he had grown from a skinny child into a devastatingly handsome youth. He seemed pleased to see me and, pint glass in hand, more affable than I'd ever known him. We left the Cockney Pride and embarked on a pub crawl that lasted till closing time. The debate about what to do then was settled when we jumped over the back wall of a drinking club and stole a crate of beer to drink back at my latest home three miles out of the city in Llanrhummey. I was sharing a flat with two guys I'd met some weeks before in the Blue Anchor: Howard was in his forties and bore a resemblance to Frankie Howerd and Paul was in his late twenties and made his living from an ice-cream van he drove round the estates. He always had young boys helping him and often brought them home for sex.

Howard and Paul made themselves scarce when I got back with Patrick and his two friends. Both of them knew a lot about Patrick as he'd always been my favourite topic of conversation. We sat in the comfortable lounge listening to music and drinking out of the bottles we'd just stolen. Around one o'clock, Patrick's two friends said they were off to look up a couple of girls they knew and did he want to come? He wasn't very interested so they left the two of us on our own together. The sofa in the lounge turned down into a bed and without anything being said I knew Patrick was staying. Perhaps it was the drink which took away my fear because in no time at all we were both undressed and in bed together. His naked body looked and felt even better than I'd imagined, making the three years I'd waited to hold him close more than worth it. I'd never felt so happy but it didn't last long. After a couple of minutes Patrick began to sober up. Soon after that he got up and dressed saying it was time he got home.

I only saw him again twice. The first time was in town when he crossed the road to avoid me, the second he was out walking with a young girl on his arm. Something inside me gave up hoping. Suddenly the three years I'd spent living in Cardiff seemed liked wasted circles. I wanted to be alive and in love and not have to sneak into places like the Blue Anchor in case anyone saw me. There was only one place I knew I might feel comfortable: London.

CHAPTER 12

I TOLD NOBODY I WAS LEAVING AND TOOK LITTLE WITH ME other than memories: a blue plastic laundry bag of clothes, a radio stolen from Paul and Howard's flat and twenty pounds in my pocket. The place for chickens in London at the time was the *Le Duce* club so when my train pulled into Paddington I made straight for Soho. I was the first customer through the door. The heavyweight black man who took my money noticed my bag and stored it away in his kiosk. He asked if I'd be staying long in London and smiled. Inside the club Marvin Gaye's 'I Heard It Through the Grapevine' was blasting out from two giant speakers at one end of the low-ceilinged room. The small dance area in front of the dj was lit by the luminous green glow from the tropical fish tank set in the side of the wall. I thought I'd come to the wrong place but around midnight the club began to fill rapidly. There were a lot of young boys but also some older men too. One of these, in a black velvet suit and tortoise-shell glasses, offered to buy me a drink and said his name was Maurice. I was impressed when he introduced me to his companion John Baldry, a blues singer with a recent number-one record in the charts. When Maurice learnt I had nowhere to live he said I could stay with him for a while.

I was up early for my first full day in London. Maurice had been very understanding when he realized he didn't turn me on and had let me sleep. My first priority was to find a job and I knew I would also have to find a room. That afternoon I was in sole charge of a cart selling hamburgers and cold fizzy drinks. My wages were to be paid on results at the end of each day. I set up shop next to the Palace Theatre in Shaftesbury Avenue. Danny la Rue was starring there and I thought I might get a glimpse of him going in through the stage door.

It was a warm spring afternoon and I was just taking some money for a coke when two men rushed past, one of them almost knocking my customer to the ground. A loud clanging bell began to ring. It was joined by the sound of approaching police sirens. Within a minute the area was swamped. An ambulance swerved to a halt, its back doors opened and a bald man with blood all over his white shirt was helped out of the theatre's ticket office and driven away to hospital. It must have been a robbery or something. I felt exhilarated. I was living in a place where almost anything might happen.

Finding a room was a depressing experience. I walked for miles looking at cards in shop windows but almost all of them insisted 'No Irish, No coloured'. Eventually I found an attic room I could afford in an Indian household in Streatham.

It was a surprisingly risky business selling hamburgers – at any moment I was at risk of being arrested and fined for illegal street-trading. I felt more secure after starting work as a kitchen porter in an Oxford Street health restaurant but two weeks later I was back in Cardiff. I had missed the place terribly and couldn't stop thinking about all the people I'd left behind. One evening I stopped to chat with a woman who ran a popcorn kiosk. She asked if I would look after it while she used the loo but as soon as she left I searched through her handbag and took the cash from her purse and the money from the till, almost seventy pounds.

Cardiff was a disappointment after the hectic bustle of London. I stayed for two days trying to impress people with the money in my pocket and new clothes on my back before heading back to London. Still comparatively rich, I spent a few days touring the various gay pubs, dancing through the night at *Le Duce* with the help of purple hearts. When *Le Duce* closed its doors at six, there was always a group from the club to tag along with to someone's flat or bedsit for a come-down party. This involved sprawling around on floors and chairs with a group of people united by the depressing effects of the drugs wearing off.

Walking in Piccadilly one evening, where the male rent scene was busiest, a tall expensively dressed man stopped me and asked if I had the time. He was tall, thin and in his forties with almost white hair and a Scandinavian accent. I smiled and said yes to his invitation to take me to dinner. He was staying at the Park Lane Hilton and suggested we eat in the rooftop restaurant. The deference of the waiter and the opulent surroundings made me feel quite sophisticated, the only minor irritant being that I had to reassure my host several times that I would suck his cock when we went back to his room. To make conversation I asked the Scandinavian what he did for a living. He didn't explain very clearly but it was plain that he travelled all over the world. A lot of his time had been spent in Lagos so I told him that was where my father lived and that he had come to this country as the son of a chief to study medicine. He asked me his name. 'Bayo', I said. 'Doctor Ade Bayo?' was his immediate response. 'I know him very well.' He knew a lot more and for the rest of the meal he filled in chunks of my history which had never been told to me. My father and his family held an eminent position in African society and were known throughout the country. Apparently I had an uncle who was a lawyer and playboy of such repute that folk songs were sung about his various affairs. The Scandinavian asked if I would like him to inform my father of my whereabouts. I said I would, but I didn't believe finding him could be such a simple matter. After the meal, my host took me back to his suite. While he sat whistling happily in the bath I rifled through his pockets. A few moments later I was in the lift and leaving the hotel a few pounds richer.

If I had a home in London it was *Le Duce*. After twelve months I was almost a permanent fixture. I made it my business to get on with the owners and eventually I worked there, either on the door or playing the music. I had the keys so I didn't have to worry about a roof over my head – I was quite comfortable sleeping on one of the benches during the day. My expenses were paid for by selling blue amphetamine pills I obtained from some villains from North London. The supply was unlimited and I soon built up a regular clientele.

I had arrived in London unsure, shy and grieving for Patrick. A year later, I felt completely different: I felt attractive. There was never any difficulty in picking up good looking boys on the gay scene. Everywhere I went it was known I had a pocketful of pills. Conversation was easy: 'Would you like a drink?' 'Some Blues?' and, finally, 'Do you want to sleep with me?' I loved the sense of power which being a drug dealer gave me. Everybody wanted to be my friend. One of my customers, a weekend speed freak, was so concerned to be seen in my company he gave me an American Oldsmobile with blue tinted windows in an attempt to curry favour. He gave me the keys while apologizing for the heavy petrol consumption. I didn't care – with my ankle-length mock fur coat and fancy jewellery, the car complimented my Mr Cool image.

My career in pushing pills was brought to an abrupt halt late one night. Drunk and hallucinating from the effect of too many blues in my system, I was driving my car along a narrow street near to the club and not making a very good job of steering. Half awake, I crashed into one car parked by the kerb. The noise of tearing metal made me swing the wheel wildly to the right, tearing the paintwork and denting the side of another parked on the opposite side of the road. Pulling the car back on course I scraped alongside what looked like a Rolls Royce or Bentley. By the time I reached the next corner I'd left a line of damaged cars which stretched the entire length of the street. The deafening noise brought me to my senses. I knew there must have been witnesses and as my car was such a familiar sight in the West End it wouldn't be long before the police were onto me. I abandoned the car realizing I would have to keep away from *Le Duce* as well. The only place I could think of to lie low was the bed sit of a girl called Penny who lived in Hammersmith.

Penny was one of my customers. She loved speeding and dancing the night away at *Le Duce*. She had dark Romany looks and wore tops which made the most of her voluptuous breasts. I'd often ended up at her bedsit for a come-down party but never paid her much attention. Soon after first meeting her I realized she found me attractive and for that reason I knew she would put me up for a while. My only fear was where I would sleep: apart from the floor there was only one bed. I was relieved on the first night when Penny took the initiative and placed a bolster down the middle to avoid the risk of touching while we slept.

After several weeks I realized that I liked living with Penny. We shared the same interest in pretty boys and, at another level, it felt comfortable living and being seen out with an attractive girl. Penny soon tired of the gay boys she seduced into her bed and would often pass them down to me where I was sleeping on the floor.

It soon became obvious that Penny and I would have to move to a larger room. We also needed more privacy. The landlord and residents at the house in Hammersmith were getting uptight with the steady stream of early morning visitors. The final straw came when the landlord arrived to pick up the rent and to empty the meter one morning. He knocked on the door and a dozen of so exotically dressed friends had to slip out the back window to hide in the small overgrown garden. They must have been seen because shortly after they all climbed back into our room, the landlord returned and opened the door without warning. He went berserk and began shouting in a Polish accent that we were turning his house into a brothel. Penny tried to pacify his rage with the invention we had all met up before setting out for a picnic in the country but the landlord wasn't a bit convinced. 'At eight o'clock in the morning?' he screamed. Then the old Irish couple who lived in the front room and Mrs Owewee the African lady from the first floor joined in.

'She's got all sorts in there,' protested the Irish man dressed only in trousers and a string vest. 'I'm sick of them all,' he complained. 'She's got men dressed as women. Women dressed as men. Poofs and queers. They come here at all hours, waking us up.'

Mrs Owewee chipped in with the observation that it was these strange people who stole the toilet paper from the first floor loo and replaced it with pages torn from the telephone book.

We moved from Hammersmith to Earl's Court, the centre of London's gay ghetto. It was another bedsit but much larger. I'd come across a false driving licence and used it to secure a job driving a van which delivered meals from a Belgravian restaurant to local affluent homes. The bulk of the work took place during the evening and around midnight I would meet up with Penny at *Masquerade* in Earl's Court to spend whatever tips I had made. With purple hearts not so easily available, we began to discover the wonders of LSD.

The first time I took it was a revelation. I discovered that locked away inside me was a world of staggering beauty. I thought at first I had paid ten shillings for a dud trip but walking along the street half an hour later I was transfixed by a neon sign outside a Chinese fish and chip shop. I must have stood there for an hour amazed at the silver fish swimming, in the neon glow, watching how the silver scales caught the light of the sun and reflected into the deep blue sea.

My affection for *Le Duce* was transferred to *Masquerade*. If you had the money you could rub shoulders in the club's restaurant with the up-and-coming stars of the entertainment world. I loved sitting there with my latest pick up who couldn't fail to be impressed by the faces he recognized and who knew me to say hello. Delivering meals to wealthy customers didn't pay well enough for such extravagance but I also had money coming in from other sources. One of the most reliable was an arrangement I had with two bent CID officers. I'd first met them when I was pushing pills – they had scared off another pusher encroaching on my territory. Since then we had a regular scam which involved me stealing a colour television set from the lounge of one of the many small hotels in the area and selling it for a song to someone more or less respectable. The following day the customer would be visited by two policemen acting on information that they were in the possession of stolen goods. Terrified of arrest, the customer was more than willing to pay a bribe (which was split three ways) in return for agreeing to give back the telly on the understanding nothing more would be said.

My two police officers also appropriated any drugs which were seized in raids which they passed on to me to sell on commission. Needless to say it was often me who provided the addresses most profitable to visit.

I had been living with Penny for six months when she had to go into hospital for a major operation on her hands which were badly scarred when she had tripped over, stoned out of her mind, and grabbed the bars of an electric fire in an attempt to break her fall. Her parents had insisted that after her discharge she should convalesce with them in South Africa. Penny didn't want to leave but I allayed her fears by promising to pay the rent on our room and to be there when she returned. She was further reassured by the fact I had been seeing Phillip, a boy who she judged to be both sensible and honest.

Phillip was twenty and small for his age. He was different to any of the boys I usually ended up with. The gift of the gab which comes with amphetamines had made an impression. After meeting me he had dumped his girlfriend and embarked on a new gay life. It felt like Patrick in reverse: I was Phillip's first love and I knew he would do anything I asked.

On New Year's Eve I was broke and depressed. There were still a few expensive tickets left for the dinner and celebrations being held later that night at *Masquerade* and I wanted to be there. Directly behind the house I lived in stood one which looked unoccupied. I waited for the late afternoon darkness before snooping around the rear and discovering a window I was able to force. It was my first burglary, but it was like a clock being turned back. Standing in the empty house I might have been back in the private quarters of the children's home superintendent. I felt a tense but delicious fear violating the space where other people lived. I chose the bedroom first, instinctively, as if I could sense where money might be hidden. It was a young couple's home I thought – there was a poster of David Bowie on the wall and a guitar shoved under the bed. The money was hidden under a sheet of newspaper lining a drawer. It seemed like I knew it was there even before I found it. There was too much to stand and count but back in the safety of my own room I laid the banknotes out on the bed and counted a little over five hundred pounds. I'd never had so much money – it was like a great fortune. Burglary had everything going for it: danger, excitement and a feeling like being on LSD. I was really looking forward to the coming New Year.

One thing I'd often imagined was living in a place I wouldn't feel awkward inviting someone back to. It was one thing to impress a boy in a club with the money in my pocket but it was a bit of an embarrassment when my home turned out to be a single room. I would explain it was only temporary but it always sounded unconvincing. With the bulk of the money I had stolen I decided to improve my image by moving into a two-bedroomed basement flat in Hammersmith.

News of my improved circumstances spread rapidly and soon my new home became a resting place for half a dozen good looking boys. One of these had a flair for forging signatures. We worked well together. I stepped up the rate of houses I broke into and settled for half the takings from the credit cards and cheque books.

Another of the boys made money by selling his body. It was his idea that we join forces to rob one of his punters who owned a lot of expensive jewellery. We called on the victim in the early evening. Alan had telephoned to let him know that he was calling round to his flat with a good-looking black guy. Inside the luxurious apartment we were both handed tumblers of scotch and dry ginger which I sipped politely. Alan put his on the glass topped table in front of him, turned on our host sitting next to him and crashed his fist into the side of his unsuspecting jaw. The punter gave a strangled scream and cried out, 'Take anything you want.' Before searching his flat we tied him up with the electric flex ripped from the television set. Alan kidded him that I'd killed before and the punter, an effeminate man in his early thirties, shrieked. 'Take my jewellery – it's hidden under the towels in the bathroom.' We didn't stay long. A cruising taxi picked us up, Alan carrying three mink coats while I held the small brown jewellery case.

Back at my flat we forced it open, glittering jewellery winked and sparkled from its red velvet bed. A typewritten inventory inside the case listed the insurance value at more than twenty thousand pounds. Under a false bottom of the box was an added bonus: three hundred pounds in brand new fivers.

Alan and I were both keen to celebrate. We had graduated from pinching pennies to thousands of pounds. A taxi took us to a Park Lane hotel. From there we moved on to *Masquerade*. I thought if there was anyone beautiful in the place that evening they couldn't help but be impressed to learn where I would be sleeping that night. I meant to enjoy myself but first I telephoned my two policemen friends. I explained in a cryptic fashion that I needed their help to find a reliable fence for the jewellery. I also wanted to inform them anonymously that at a certain address in Belgravia our victim could be found bound and gagged. We arranged to meet the following evening and I left the phone box for an evening of playing millionaire.

It was a good night at the club. Within minutes I was entertaining a young Scottish boy. After dinner he agreed to come back to the hotel – I couldn't wait to show off the jewellery which I had hidden under the sheets at the foot of the bed, but when I went to get them, they were missing. I immediately assumed one of the hotel staff was responsible. For some reason I imagined that the police would come crashing through the door at any moment. I had to get out of the hotel as quickly as possible so I roused Alan from the room next door and we left.

I felt awful for days. I couldn't stop thinking about the fortune I'd lost. Alan disappeared to his parents' in the East End but on the grapevine I heard that he was out every night spending money like water. It took a while for me to realize that after the robbery Alan had robbed me but I wasn't going to let him get away with it. I made arrangements to meet with my two policemen and after telling them the whole story they promised to 'break his fucking legs'. Their anger was fuelled by the profit they would have made from the sale of the jewels. That evening I sat in the back of a CID car as we toured the West End searching for Alan. Up front my two policemen kept promising we would find 'the little shit'.

He wasn't that difficult to find. A few minutes after midnight he was locked in a cell at the police station. My policemen friends recovered some of the property which they sold and with my cut I decided to take a holiday – I knew that it would have to be France.

I decided to take Phillip with me for a weekend in Paris. We were due to catch an early-morning flight from Heathrow but at four o'clock in the morning there was a loud knock on the front door of my flat. It was the police. They arrested me for the suspected theft of an electric typewriter which I had stolen as a favour to a friend who was setting up a secretarial service in Soho. Brixton was my first taste of a London prison and I didn't like it one bit. I arrived with a group of other prisoners in the late afternoon and was kept waiting in a large holding cell for hours before the tedious process of being searched, examined and labelled with a number. It was dark when I eventually got to the main wing. A prison officer unlocked a cell door and motioned me inside. An ugly voice from the bottom bunk bed informed my escort, 'I ain't sharing no cell with a nigger'. Standing with a bed roll under one arm and a plastic pot in my other hand I wished the ground would swallow me up. The screw seemed equally embarrassed and found a more congenial place for me to sleep.

I was held on remand for three months. Phillip visited me regularly and made life more bearable by bringing with him cigarettes and other small luxuries. One Saturday afternoon he turned up with Penny who had just returned from South Africa. I felt bad because I had promised to keep the bedsit while she was away but she put my mind at ease when she explained she had a live-in job as a chambermaid at an Earl's Court hotel. Chatting together but separated by reinforced glass, we told each other I would soon be out. I hoped for a suspended sentence or even possibly probation. I didn't tell Phillip or Penny that in addition to the charge of stealing the typewriter I'd also admitted to several other burglaries.

Later that night I mentally rehearsed what I would say to the Judge if I got the chance. How would he feel if he'd been robbed of his childhood? It was all very well him sitting in judgement over the possessions I'd stolen, but who was ever going to say sorry for what had been stolen from me? Would anyone be punished for the distress they had caused me? Surely the Judge would understand that the reason I stole was because please and thank you were alien concepts to me. As my silent soliloquy gathered momentum the make-believe Judge was joined by an audience of the whole world. They nodded their heads in agreement with my argument. When the Judge dismissed me from the dock a free man, loud applause swept through the court. On the actual day in court things turned out a bit differently and I was sentenced to eighteen months.

Wormwood Scrubs was dirty and overcrowded. There

were men serving sentences which ranged from days to thirty years. At my reception interview, the wing governor said I could expect to be in the Scrubs for six weeks before being transferred to another prison. Most of this time was spent banged up for twenty-four hours a day with two other blokes in a cramped and smelly cell. One of these was a frail old man in his late sixties. On the day he moved in with his bed roll he showed me bruises he'd been given by two young blokes he'd been sharing a cell with. A lump came to my throat as I heard how he'd been bullied and had his food taken from him. I knew I was likely to be transferred to a relatively cushy semi-open prison, but I thought I would rather stay where I was to give the old man a measure of protection.

I arrived at Northeye Prison in the summer of 1972. The complex of wooden buildings had once served as military barracks and I was reminded of the Village homes at Barkingside. After being allocated a bed in one of the dormitories I was put to work linking small chains onto silver plated Brut medallions which hung round the necks of the dark green bottles of aftershave. When asked, 'What are you in for?' I invented a glamorous history for myself. I let it be known I was a man of substance who had come unstuck in one of many large-scale cheque frauds. I didn't want anyone to know I was just another unsuccessful burglar. After linking silver chains together for three weeks, I applied for a job in the kitchen not because I was particularly interested in the catering side but I wanted to get to sleep in the kitchen dorm next to a blond boy called John who worked as a baker. He was cool to me at first but I persisted with charm. With a soft warm body to lie beside at night my hankering for the gay world of London began to fade.

It was at Northeye I first discovered what it felt like to be understood. Mr Mottram, one of the resident probation officers, called me up to his office once a week and for a couple of hours I was free to talk about anything I chose. I began to understand the rewards which came from self-reflection. For the first time I experienced the relief which came from trusting another person with the parts of myself I hated. I talked endlessly about the father I had never seen and described my secret dream in which he appeared without warning and whisked me off to a world in which I belonged. Another frequent subject of discussion centred on my attraction to other young men. I explained over and over how guilty I felt and over the weeks Mr Mottram helped me to take a less harsh attitude to my sexuality. The prison became my home. I had friends. I wasn't really looking forward to my release but twelve months later I walked through the prison gates and linked arms with Penny who was waiting for me.

With the money Penny had saved from her chambermaid job and my discharge grant we had just enough to put down a deposit on a large double bedsit overlooking Regent's Park. There were other immediate expenses to cover so I went to call on the friend who had given my address to the police when they questioned him about the stolen typewriter. I knew he would feel uneasy about what had happened and I let him believe I was still contemplating some form of revenge. I asked him for an indefinite loan to get me back on my feet. He was anxious to please.

On my first night of freedom Penny and I revisited old haunts and ending up at *Masquerade* in Earl's Court. I'd expected to find the place as I'd known it twelve months before but there were so few faces I recognized I felt like a stranger in the place. Even worse was seeing the new fresh young faces on the scene pass me by with scarcely a glance. Shortly before the club closed Penny got into conversation with a pot-bellied man in his thirties who said he was a freelance journalist. He bought us both drinks and offered a lift home in his car to Regent's Park. He must have been very tired because he soon fell asleep on the plastic couch. Much later while he and Penny slept, I crept from my bed and took fifty pounds from his wallet. I was already up to my old tricks and I knew that if I wasn't careful I would soon end up back inside. I thought it best to find a job.

Telling a pack of lies to a friendly personnel manager resulted in a position of trainee supermarket manager. The wages were quite good and I looked forward to a more settled life where I would be in charge of my own store. I spent the first week of training filling shelves in the Bayswater branch and then was sent to one of the other shops in Holland Park to share the responsibility of management with another young chap. Although I worked conscientiously for the first couple of weeks, I couldn't put out of my mind the hundreds of pounds which had to be counted and banked every day. One Sunday evening, an area manager called and tore me off a strip in front of a shop full of customers after finding a rotten piece of celery on the vegetable display. He warned me that if it happened again I could lose my job. As soon as he'd gone I phoned Penny and told her to pack our bags. I said we were going on holiday and she could choose where we went.

We had almost two thousand pounds and in a few hours we had checked into a five-star Amsterdam hotel, my first time abroad. Together we visited the gay places we'd heard so much about but we were both depressed when we returned in the early hours of the morning to our hotel. In Earl's Court we could have had twice as much fun. It didn't help not being able to score any speed so, before settling down to sleep, we decided to move on the next day to Morocco.

Casablanca was hot and the air we breathed on stepping out of the plane tasted sweet. We caught a rickety bus which spluttered its way to the city centre. One of the first sights to greet us was a forlorn group of people in Arab dress looking down at what seemed a dead body spread-eagled in the middle of the road. Suddenly Casablanca was where we didn't want to be. We were both feeling tired after the flight and a night of booze in Amsterdam but we pressed on by train to Tangiers.

I had visions of arriving in Tangiers and discovering the world I had read about in books: a place where bronze-skinned Arab boys offered their bodies for love. Penny sitting next to me on the train was beginning to worry about the future and what we were going to do when we returned to London. I told her to relax and counted out a hundred pounds. Whatever the future held she at least had some money to fall back on.

Tangiers didn't improve Penny's mood. She didn't like squatting over a black hole and longed for conventional English toilet seats. More depressing were the hordes of young children who followed us begging for coppers whenever we visited the market. I wouldn't have minded the Arab boys' attentions if they had been a little older and although most of them spoke English they were still too young for me to ask where we had to go to find the local gay scene. We spent the week in Tangiers drinking beer and smoking hashish we bought in the Casbah.

Neither of us was very happy so we decided to head back home – it was the most enjoyable part of our holiday. The plane was supposed to pick up other passengers from Gibraltar but our departure from the Rock was postponed by rough weather. The airline put us up for the night in a luxury hotel and while Penny sang in a deep hot bath I did the tourist bit, taking a cable car for a closer look at the island's baboon population. It was the first time since leaving London I felt I really was on holiday.

London in April was cold wet and windy and Morocco suddenly seemed a lot more attractive. I still had about three hundred pounds left, the bulk of which went on settling Penny and I into another dingy bedsit, this time in Baron's Court. Apart from an afghan coat each and some junk Arab jewellery we had nothing to show for the money we had spent. Our living conditions were worse than the bedsit in Hammersmith where I had first gone to live with Penny. I still had a few pounds in my pocket so, to cheer us both up, I took Penny for a meal at *Masquerade*. It was buzzing with talk of how the owners of the place had been tied up and robbed of property worth thousands of pounds. They stopped at my table and gave me an account of what had happened. In an expansive and solicitous mood, I offered to track down the culprits, hinting I had contacts at all levels of the underworld. Swept along in an alcoholic fantasy of being hired as a private eye I promised to take on the case. As a special concession I agreed that I would only charge for my expenses which in turn would be paid on results.

I was up early the next morning. I needed to feel the part, so I stopped at a newsagent to buy a notebook and pen. I had one slender lead – one of the robbers was known to the victims. Some weeks previously he'd been invited into their home as a pick up. He left behind him a scratch pad on which there was a telephone number. I dialled it and with a little deception discovered the phone was in Clapham. A few minutes later I was knocking on the door. The middle-aged woman who opened it was very co-operative when she learnt I was investigating a serious crime – I think she assumed I was a policeman. When I described the young man I was looking for, she was able to tell me immediately he was the boyfriend of a girl who used to rent a room in her house. The girl had moved away but at least I had a name and the information she might have been admitted to the psychiatric hospital in Tooting.

An hour later I was sitting at the girlfriend's bedside

allowing her to think I was another hospital social worker. She seemed quite stable and chatted easily about her boyfriend and the baby she was going to have. I knew the case was all but solved when I learnt that the boyfriend would be visiting her later that evening. I telephoned the *Masquerade*'s owners and gave them the information. They were surprised and delighted and passed the information to the police immediately. I felt quite proud with my performance – in a couple of hours I had solved a major crime. Sipping champagne in the club that evening I learnt that the robber had been arrested and would be appearing in court the next day.

A few days later it was my turn to be arrested. An employee of the supermarket I'd robbed spotted me waiting for a tube at Earl's Court station. Two constables came up to me and asked if they could have a word. At the police station I signed a statement admitting my guilt and was locked in a cell.

During the first week on remand I received an unexpected letter from a boy I'd met shortly before my arrest. He had discovered my whereabouts from Penny and wanted to know if there was anything he could do to help. When I wrote back saying I would like him to visit me, he came the following day bringing with him cigarettes and food. I was surprised by the warmth of his smiles because when we had last met I'd been wearing an expensive jumper which I'd stolen from his flat. Chris said he had been in touch with a solicitor on my behalf who thought he could get me bail. There was also a chance of escaping another prison sentence by pointing out in mitigation that it had been a cruel temptation to be placed in charge of so much money so soon after being released from prison. At the next magistrates' hearing I was given bail on condition I live at Chris's house. It was mid-summer and it was bliss to be out of the sweltering hot remand cells of Brixton.

Chris, a blond-haired boy with blue eyes, was a month older than me. He worked as a window dresser for a Bond Street shop and his artistic flair was reflected in the comfort of his flat. He reminded me that his place was my home too and taking him at his word I turned my thoughts to a longer cherished dream.

I found what I was looking for at Battersea dogs' home. I wasn't sure how Chris would react so I left George, a scruffy wire-haired mongrel, in the hall while I prepared the ground. I asked him if a friend of mine who was homeless could stay for a few days. His face fell – he'd been looking forward to a weekend with just the two of us. He agreed reluctantly and I went out to fetch George. I could see the relief on Chris's face when my friend turned out to have four legs instead of two. George and I had passed the first hurdle.

In the morning we took the dog for a walk along the river at Putney. I could sense that Chris didn't like George much and when I pressed him he admitted to feeling embarrassed being seen with such a low-bred animal. He said if I wanted a dog so much why didn't I go with him to the pet department at Harrods and get a proper dog? Which meant one with a pedigree. Walking home with George scampering ahead I agreed that Chris could take him to the police station as a stray. I wouldn't go with him.

My feelings for Chris were mixed. He had grown tired and disillusioned with the gay scene and wanted someone to settle down with permanently. I liked living in his flat – the comfortable furniture, classical music and dinner served with wine – but another part of me felt trapped and wanted to be with Penny with the irregular meals and chocolate wrappers discarded in the dust under the bed. I knew I was obligated to stay with Chris at least until my court case was over, and now there was also Sasha to consider. Chris and I had been to Harrods and I was the owner of a four-month-old red setter bitch. I lavished so much attention on Sasha it seemed to make Chris jealous. The solution we agreed on was for him to have his own dog so we went back to Harrods and brought home another red setter which he called Merlin.

In October I was defended at the Crown Court by a black barrister who spoke eloquently and convinced the Judge I had turned over a new leaf. He explained how I was working as a motorcycle messenger for a West End film company and how much of my spare time was taken up training with an athletic club I'd joined. I had been very worried about what would happen to Sasha if I was sent down so I was very grateful when the Judge gave me a suspended sentence and placed me on probation.

Chris often used to speak about his parents who lived in Devon and one weekend they travelled up to London to visit him. I was supposed to be competing in a cross-country event but missed the coach and returned unexpectedly to the flat. I could tell from their reaction that they hadn't known I was sharing a flat with their son but after a few minutes they relaxed and we settled down to watch the afternoon racing. That evening we went out together to see a musical and over drinks I found myself quite naturally referring to Chris's parents as mum and dad. They both seemed pleased that I did. Saying goodbye to them both at the station mum leaned forward, kissed me on the cheek and whispered in my ear that she wouldn't worry quite so much now that she knew Chris had me to look after him.

I lost my job as a motorcycle messenger after taking too many days off. Out of work and living on Chris's overdraft I turned once again to burglary. I broke into an antique shop and carried away two plastic bin-liners filled with Art Nouveau bric-a-brac. Chris wasn't happy when he discovered what I'd done but after some persuasion agreed to help me sell some pieces. We raised enough cash to cover our immediate needs but the following day, without telling Chris, I took a couple of silver pieces to a shop in the West End. The stall holder asked me to wait for a couple of minutes while he popped out to the bank. He returned with a uniformed constable. As usual I admitted my guilt at the police station and there was no objection to bail. Back home I convinced Chris that the only way we could stay together would be by running away. With a suspended sentence hanging over me we had to get out of London.

Chris's parents lived on a neat council estate in Plymouth. We travelled on the night train and were just in time to catch dad as he left for work. Mum was overjoyed to see us and over a sizzling breakfast of bacon and eggs told me that the house was my home for as long as I wanted.

Chris and I had little money so we took the first jobs we could find at a hotel near the seafront. Chris had to dress in a page-boy uniform and carry suitcases or pots of tea. I was more fortunate. Producing a fake licence, I got a job driving the courtesy cab between the hotel and railway station. The first day of work was so humiliating for Chris he said he wasn't going back. I kept my job for a week before being stopped for speeding and failing a Breathalyser test. My fake driving licence passed initial inspection by the arresting officer but I wondered how safe I would be once the case came to court. Would I be identified as having jumped bail in London?

I reckoned I had about six weeks' breathing space so I found a job as a hospital porter. I only worked there for a week. Collecting my wages, I left the hospital with a collection of cheque books and credit cards which I had filched from lockers in the doctors' changing rooms. We left Plymouth – and mum, dad, Sasha and Merlin – on the Saturday afternoon.

Chris and I spent a couple of days back in London, making money from the stolen cheques I cashed at various shops and banks. We both realized it would be risky staying in the capital so we moved to Brighton into a small bedsit near the Seven Dials. The holiday season was in full swing and we both found it easy to get jobs. Chris started work as a window dresser at one of the town's largest stores while I landed a position dispensing drinks behind the bar in one of Brighton's trendiest restaurants. I endeared myself to the two young proprietors when I chased and caught one of a number of young men who had done a runner from the restaurant to avoid paying the bill.

I liked living in Brighton but Chris wasn't so happy. When he came home from work I was just leaving for the evening shift so he spent a lot of his time alone. When we were actually together we always seemed to be squabbling. I was drinking too much to numb the constant fear of being on the run. I was also spending time on my own in the gay clubs and lying to Chris about where I'd been. I needed Chris for the security he gave me but I felt a smouldering resentment being tied to him and unable to find the boy who would make my life complete. I could never forget the reason we were together was because he had rescued me from prison. At times I felt like George at Battersea dogs' home waiting for a new owner.

We had been living in Brighton for a couple of months when Chris caught a train to Plymouth to fetch Sasha and Merlin. While he was gone I lost my job. I wasn't exactly sacked but thought it best if I left. I stole a bulging purse from one of the waitresses but the theft was discovered almost immediately. I could feel the eyes of the staff flickering towards me, as if everyone in the restaurant knew I was guilty but was too embarrassed to make an outright accusation. When the place closed for the night I made an excuse about having to visit a sick relative and apologized for not being able to give a week's notice. I'm not sure who felt most relieved about my leaving, the proprietor or me.

A few days later I applied for a job at a bingo hall as a part-time runner whose responsibility was to check the cards of potential winners. The manager was a kind old gentleman who listened to my story about moving from London to marry a local girl and suggested I might like the more challenging position of full-time trainee assistant manager. Chris wasn't happy about me finding another job which involved evening work and the rows got worse. The combination of his discontent and the safe in the bingo hall office determined our next move. I put it to Chris that with minimum risk I could steal enough cash to finance a move to a larger town where we could find a decent home to live in, somewhere with a garden for Sasha and Merlin. Reluctantly, he agreed. I worked at the bingo hall for a month and then on a Sunday evening while the manager, resplendent in evening dress, warmed up the housewives I sneaked into his office and emptied the contents of the safe into a duffle bag. Chris had left for London earlier that day with the dogs and our belongings and a minicab was waiting to drive me up to meet him. We stayed overnight in a five-star hotel and while we waited for room service we counted the money: almost three thousand pounds, more than enough to pay for a fresh start. We debated the wisdom of staying hidden in London but decided to head for Manchester where Chris had been a student.

The city had a smell of damp bricks. It was populated with people from my past – somehow I knew that this was where my grandmother once lived. With money in our pockets it was easy to find somewhere to live and for the first time in months Chris seemed happy. He loved the detached cottage we moved into and shopping for new clothes and luxuries for our new home swept away the memories of life on the run.

We both realized the money wouldn't last indefinitely so Chris started work in a shop and I went back to school for six weeks to learn the academic side of becoming second man to the driver of a British Rail train. The lessons ended just before Christmas. All I seemed to have learnt was how to place detonators on the track to warn approaching trains of any obstructions on the line. I tried to absorb the instructions on how to start up the trains' steam boilers which provided the carriage heating but it was all so complicated I gave up. My first shift was due to start at midnight but with thick snow on the ground and a biting wind I stayed at home. To placate Chris's protests I promised to look for alternative employment.

Instead of visiting the job centre or scanning the local newspaper I turned to full-time burglary. Chris thought I was working behind a bar during the evening but in fact I was walking the streets searching for unoccupied houses to break into. I was rarely fooled by strategically placed lights behind closed curtains. Somehow I just knew whether a house was safe to enter or not. On New Year's Eve I broke into what must have been my fortieth house and found a small safe disguised as a bedside cabinet. It was too heavy to carry more than a few yards so I borrowed a wheelbarrow from the garden shed to carry the safe away but going through the front gate the barrow tipped over and the safe fell onto the pavement with an almighty crash. A curtain in the house next door was pulled back and then a middle-aged man walked down his garden path towards me. I never went out on burglaries without having a few drinks first to give me confidence and that night I was fairly drunk. I ignored the neighbour, struggled to lift the safe back into the barrow. The man helpfully held it steady while I loaded the safe. As I tottered off down the street he called after me, 'Happy New Year'.

It seemed like it might be. After sweating with a chisel for several hours the safe yielded a collection of gold sovereigns, jewellery and cash. I told Chris it had come from a one-off burglary. He was angry but the money soon settled his rage. By this time breaking into houses had become a compulsion. I knew it was just a matter of time before the police caught up with me and in fact they came to the cottage that January. The two CID officers informed me Chris was already in custody. I offered to make a full statement on condition they accept Chris had played no part in the crimes and to sweeten the bait I promised to enlighten them about scores of other offences. They seemed very pleased and let me feed and water the dogs before taking me to the police station. As the cell door slammed shut I felt an enormous weight lift from my mind. For the first time in months I had a future – in prison I would be free from Chris and, maybe, I might find the boy I had always been searching for there.

CHAPTER 13

RISLEY REMAND CENTRE, OR GRIZZLY AS IT WAS CALLED BY ITS inmates, was at its coldest during the early months of 1976 but eventually the weeks of speculation were ended when at Manchester Crown Court I was sentenced to almost five years' imprisonment. Logic had prepared me for a fairly hefty sentence but it was still a shock when it came. Even with maximum remission I would be pushing thirty by the time I got out. Chris, who had moved back to London to pick up the threads of his life, kept in touch and mum and dad had written from Devon. Whatever happened, they said, there would always be a home for me with them.

Shortly after my arrival at Strangeways, I was hauled up in front of the Governor for using abusive language towards one of his officers. It had been worth it at the time, but the seven days' isolation down the block made me think again. Being cut off from human contact terrified me. I hated counting the hours from seven in the morning till seven at night with nothing to do but sit on a wooden chair. I had only a bible for company and reading this had to be a secret otherwise I would have to face the derisive comments of the screw checking through the Judas hole in the door.

Back on the main wing I was put to work in the weavers'

shop. For £1.50 a week I tended the clattering noisy machines which turned out blue and white cloth from which prison shirts were tailored. In the evenings there were various classes as well as choir practice and Padre's hour. I wasn't motivated by any love of religion or improving my mind but by the opportunity of spending time outside the cell I shared with two others, as well as the occasional chance of hasty sex. I was constantly inventing excuses for a change of cell in order to share a bed with the latest guy who caught my eye. Many a night was passed with the glass in the Judas eye smeared with toothpaste to obscure the view of any passing screw whilst making love to the sound of Piccadilly Radio on my transistor.

One of my lovers gave me a book to read on Buddhism. I only accepted it out of politeness but was amazed to find the subject matter completely absorbing. For the first time in my life I read about the virtue of detachment. I was fascinated by the possibility of blurring the distinction between opposites and by the concept of seeing through the illusion of man-made religious structures. I was being encouraged to believe I didn't exist in reality, that if I could cease all mental thought I could be aware of my true nature. Plagued with deep guilt about my sexuality and dissatisfied with the image I had of myself, I willingly embraced escape into the Buddhist void. I began scouring the prison library for similar books and when I wasn't making love or chasing other boys I sat for hours attempting to meditate. Religion had always been about a Jesus who could never smile on a homosexual so Buddhism came as a breath of fresh air encouraging me to enquire into the meaning of life instead of saying 'thou shalt not'.

The first twelve months in Strangeways passed very slowly, so I was pleased when I was transferred to Lancaster prison which felt a bit like a holiday camp in comparison. The screws spoke civilly and didn't seem interested

118

in enforcing petty rules. You spent a far greater period outside your cell and consequently there were more opportunities to strike up sexual liaisons. I went to work sewing collars onto blue prison shirts. Wages were paid on a Friday afternoon and instead of signing for what we had earned and being handed what we chose from the canteen by a screw we were paid in actual cash. No notes though, just coins. One enterprising con from the vocational training course which taught radio and television repairs was turning out fake fifty-pence pieces made from solder which cost fifteen pence each. It was several weeks before the canteen screw tumbled to how much stock had been paid for with forged coins.

At Strangeways, probation officers were too busy to deal with any but the most urgent problems but at Lancaster things were very different. Phyllis, a large matronly woman, introduced herself on my first week in the place and offered to make herself available for a couple of hours every week if I felt like talking. I warmed to her immediately and took up her offer. She didn't say a great deal during these sessions, leaving me free to expound on any subject I chose. I could detect no duplicity in her eyes as she listened with her head angled to one side and a kind smile on her face. I felt that she cared about me as a person but not simply because she was paid to do so. Week after week I sat in her small office and relived miserable days of childhood. I spoke about Chris a great deal, blaming him for my ending up back in prison. If he hadn't lured me away from Penny, I maintained, I would still be free. Most of all I returned to my favourite complaint of never being able to find a boy I could really love.

I had been at Lancaster several months when a postcard came from one of my former cellmates at Strangeways. Tommy, a delicately framed twenty-two-year-old with wide frightened brown eyes, had just been released and

119

wanted to visit me. I had been his first lover and the experience seemed to have had quite an impact on him. I used to pass him on the landing and my instincts told me he was TBH: To Be Had. Courtship began with a gift of tobacco, then the loan of a book. From there we began walking together round the exercise yard where I rapidly impressed him with my grasp of Eastern religions.

The main thrust of my daily lectures emphasized the point that the Western mind was nothing more than a conditioned machine. This could be seen most clearly in sexual matters. It didn't take long to convince Tommy that we were all basically bisexual and, that settled, I put in for another cell change and as soon as the lights were switched off on the first night we were in bed together. I was keen to see him again and sent off a visiting order. In truth I'd almost completely forgotten the time we spent together and was more interested in what drugs he might bring when he came.

In April 1978 after serving a little over two years I was called up to see the Governor who, with a smile on his face, said I'd been granted parole. I was to be let out in three weeks, sixteen months before my sentence was officially up. There were conditions, primarily that I take up the offer from mum and dad to live with them in Devon. It was a warm spring day when I stepped through the prison gates and I was really looking forward to the train journey to Devon and the buffet car shelves stacked with cans of beer. For the first hour I sat opposite two middle-aged women who talked about their home town, Morecambe. I had to resist a strong temptation to interrupt and tell the story of how I'd been shut away for the past two years in a Buddhist monastery. Before I could open my mouth the train pulled into a station and they both left. I moved into the buffet car when it opened and fell into conversation with a fellow dedicated drinker. Over cans of brown ale bought from my discharge grant I listened to the man as he reminisced about his days in military security and how his passion for the job had cost him his wife, his children and, without explanation, his right leg which was amputated above the knee. I nodded wisely and agreed things could have been worse. By the time the train was near Plymouth I'd been invited to visit the naval base he worked at. It felt as if we were old friends so I briefly explained how I'd just got out of prison that morning. A decent interval passed before my new friend rose and went to the toilet. I didn't see him again until I caught sight of him limping hurriedly along the platform and out past the ticket collector at Plymouth station. So much for honesty, I thought as I went in search of another drink.

I needed the confidence of alcohol because I was nervous about facing mum and dad. From their letters I'd received in prison I was vaguely aware their goodwill towards me was genuine but nevertheless my lifelong cynicism made me apprehensive about the reception I'd find. I wasn't sure how to behave. I felt awkward in the prison discharge clothes I was wearing: a sports jacket and flannel trousers from a bygone fashion era. I wondered if mum and dad would recognize me – I'd been horrified during the first weeks in Strangeways to discover a small bald spot developing on the top of my head and since then it had grown bigger towards an ever-receding hairline.

Mum was playing in the garden with Sasha and Merlin when the taxi pulled up outside the house in Pennycross. Her face lit up with a wide smile when she saw me and as she led me into the house she said, 'This is your home for as long as you want it to be. Just be yourself,' Unpacking my few belongings in Chris's old bedroom I puzzled over what mum meant by 'be yourself'. She couldn't mean it was alright to be gay – what if I wanted to bring a boyfriend home for the night? I couldn't be myself. If I was she'd be bound to dislike me.

When dad came home from work he rushed into the front room, shook my hand and said how pleased he was I was home at last. After a couple of sentences about staying out of trouble he repeated what mum had said about being part of the family. The next member of the household to turn up was Anthony, Chris's eighteen-year-old brother. He introduced me to his girlfriend Lorraine and their three-year-old daughter Lian.

I didn't let it show but I wasn't that keen to talk to Chris, who was expected to call that evening. We had grown apart in the time I'd spent inside and it had been months since we last wrote to each other. I was afraid he might try to revive our relationship and I didn't want that. Besides, now I had a home where I was wanted and I didn't have to be somebody's lover to keep it. His voice on the line from London sounded warm and glad to be back in touch with me but I stayed cold and distant. I wanted to punish him. 'We did have some good times together,' he said with a pleading edge in his voice.

'You might have done,' I replied, 'but I hated every moment of it.'

I could sense his shock in the silence that followed. There was nothing else to say. I put the phone down, fixed a smile on my face and walked into the kitchen where mum was preparing the family evening meal.

With the money from my first social security payment I bought the jumper and pair of jeans I needed before venturing into the town's gay scene. On a Saturday evening I left the house in high spirits, full of optimism. By 2 a.m. when the lights in the club came up I was broke, drunk and depressed. I'd seen a few attractive boys in the club but none of them had looked at me. Walking back through the town I imagined their lack of interest was because of the clothes I was wearing. If I had a more elaborate and expensive wardrobe I'd have made more of an impression. I stopped in front of clothes shops and mentally dressed myself in the stuff on display. Walking through a neon-lit arcade I spotted a half open till in one of the shops. Hardly bothering to check if the coast was clear, I kicked and shattered the glass panel in the door, wriggled through the hole and grabbed about fifty pounds. Suddenly the evening hadn't been quite as bad.

As soon as I woke up the next morning I felt physically sick. I opened my eyes and sitting on the bedside cabinet was an accusing bundle of bank notes. The events of the previous night flashed through my mind and with the images came the fear of retribution. I couldn't believe I had behaved in such a suicidal fashion. The town's main police station was across the road from the shop I'd robbed. Anyone could have walked through the brightly lit arcade as I stood emptying the till. I thought I was possibly mad. As if I'd been asking to be caught or didn't care either way. I had a picture in my mind of mum and dad's faces. Barely home a week and arrested for burglary. They would have been devastated. I was frightened at how close I'd come to hurting them both. The next few days were hell. I jumped everytime a car passed or stopped near the house. I was terrified the police were coming to arrest me. Tommy, my boyfriend from Strangeways, provided a break from the tension and stress. He phoned to say he was driving down to Plymouth and wouldn't it be a good idea to spend a few days camping on the moors. I agreed. A few days away from Plymouth was what I needed.

On my next visit to the gay club I plucked up the courage to say hello to a boy who reminded me a lot of the love of my life, Patrick. His name was Gerald and I thought he was incredibly beautiful. Every time I looked at him I was back in Cardiff and in love. Very early in our conversation I said that it wasn't important if we didn't sleep together because I wanted him more for a friend. By the end of the evening we were talking about setting up home together one day and we arranged to meet the following Saturday.

I walked home to Pennycross believing someone found me attractive balding or not. I felt good about myself – I was eighteen again. The days to the weekend dragged slowly by but I was happy. In less than twenty-four hours I'd be with the boy I'd been searching for all my life. To pass the last evening I went to a cinema to see 'The Way We Were.' I had no idea at the effect it would have on me. I was totally absorbed and the unhappy ending left me profoundly depressed.

To lighten my mood I went for a drink. I didn't leave till closing time and I wasn't feeling any better. I didn't want to lose Gerald like the lovers in the film had lost each other. If only I had some additional money I could show Gerald how much he meant to me. On the way home I clambered over a six-foot wall, smashed a window and crawled through the hole into an office. Inside I found a huge black safe which, to my surprise, was unlocked. Before I had time to strike a match in the gloom to examine the contents I heard the sound of a siren. I got out as quick as I could, reached the six foot wall and jumped over only to find blue police uniforms waiting for me. Under normal circumstances I would have seen it as a fair cop and gone quietly but I couldn't lose Gerald so easily. Several policemen wrestled me to the pavement as I tried to force my way past them. I struggled furiously but it was no good. I was crying with frustration and the policemen laughed at the desperation of my struggle. They knew I wasn't going anywhere.

At the time I'd arranged to meet Gerald I was locked up with two others in a stiflingly warm Exeter prison cell. It was seven o'clock and we'd been given mugs of sugarless cocoa before the cell door slammed shut for the night. I imagined Gerald watching the door of the pub where we'd arranged to meet, glancing up each time it opened expecting to see me walk in. I'd never felt so utterly helpless in prison. The magistrate that morning hadn't wasted any time considering bail when he learnt I was still on parole. Behind me in the public gallery I caught a glimpse of Chris's married sister with a handkerchief to her eyes. I couldn't look at her after that. The police had obviously been to see mum and dad and the whole family must have known what I'd done. The two other blokes in the cell were cheerfully nattering about football. All I could think was that I'd lost everything, not only Gerald but mum and dad too.

I thought there had been a mistake when the next afternoon a screw unlocked the cell and told me I had a visit. It had happened before: Williams was a fairly common name. 'That's your number isnt it?' the screw asked, showing me a slip of paper. 'Follow me.' I walked into the visiting room and my heart thudded painfully when I saw Sandra and mum sitting at one of the tables waiting for me. In the expression on their faces and the look in their eyes I could see they still loved me. They hadn't come to judge, they had come because they cared. Fighting to hold back the tears, they reached out and cradled my trembling hands in their own. Mum's comforting words immediately settled some of the turmoil inside me. I asked what had dad said when he heard I'd been arrested.

'Don't worry,' said mum, 'he was a bit angry at first but he wants you back home with us as soon as possible. All the family do.'

In twenty minutes mum and Sandra wiped away much of the nightmare of the past forty-eight hours. The screw who took me back to the wing handed me a large cardboard box filled with sweets and fruit. Back in my cell I felt on top of the world: I still had a mum and dad. It was almost worth being in prison to experience the pleasure of being a privileged prisoner with a family who brought gifts no matter what I'd done.

It came as no surprise when parole was revoked which meant that with the three months for burglary I had eight months in total to serve. I thought it was about time I did something practical and applied for a painting and decorating course which involved a transfer from Exeter to Bristol prison.

I felt more at home at the new place which reminded me of Strangeways and was filled with a large percentage of West Indians. I hadn't expected to enjoy the decorating course but soon developed a sense of achievement from the new skills I was learning. Having always reckoned I was useless with my hands, I was surprised at how well I could gloss paint a door to a mirror like finish. I spent most evenings in my cell studying books from the library on psychology. I was particularly drawn to the works of Freud and his belief that adult emotional problems were a result of unresolved infantile sexuality. It seemed desperately important that I make efforts to understand myself, to construct in my mind a theoretical justification for being what I was and, if possible, to preside over my own self-analysis and healing. I kept up my reading of Buddhism too and quite fancied becoming a Buddhist monk at some point in the future. I wrote a letter to the secretary of the local Bristol association asking if anyone would visit me to discuss my aspirations. The reply said yes, if the prison provided transport.

The last week of my sentence was a tense one. A lad on the wing had made a formal complaint to the governor of assault by one of the screws. To back up his claim he schooled several of us in the fiction that we had witnessed him being slapped in the face. When it was my turn to be questioned I told the governor I hadn't seen anything definite and didn't want to get involved – I was going home and didn't want to be on a charge of making malicious allegations myself. The governor seemed pleased with my response and thanked me for being honest. The day before my release I was back in front of him again for being in possession of an unauthorized object, a gold earring I'd bought with some tobacco. The addition to my appearance had been spotted by an eagle-eyed screw who smiled as he said, 'You're nicked.' I made a grovelling apology to the governor who let me off with a caution and the advice I was sailing close to the wind if I wanted to be released in the morning.

Arriving back at Pennycross was just like the last time I'd got out of prison. Dad gave a repeat performance of his brief lecture on the wisdom of staying out of trouble while the rest of the family simply let it be known they were glad I was home again. I was determined to make a real go of my life and within a week was working as a painter for one of the largest contracting firms in Plymouth. I made a reasonable job of the first two houses I was sent to paint and my third task was undercoating and glossing the woodwork of a cricket pavilion.

On Saturday evenings, wages in pocket, I went to look for Gerald. I tried the clubs and pubs but he had obviously moved on. Whenever I was out late I made sure to catch a taxi home, not wanting to risk my old compulsion to kick shop windows in. At home when the house was empty because mum and dad had gone to the Cherry Tree for an evening drink, I loved pottering about the small neat kitchen preparing a surprise late supper for their giggly return home. If dad went out with his mates I'd keep mum company in front of the television, sharing a half-bottle of gin and a chinese take-away. The only time I felt uncomfortable was when I came home from work. As I approached the house a fear would sweep over me that mum or dad would open the front door and say, 'We don't want you here anymore.' Once I stepped inside the fear would disappear until the next day.

The pavilion painting job was almost finished and as I washed out my brushes I wondered what the weekend ahead would bring. A cricket match was in progress on the green outside and during the afternoon I'd been debating with myself whether or not it was worth checking through the pockets of the cricketers' clothes. It wasn't the risk of being caught which deterred me – I was confident of getting away with that part. My reluctance came from the certain knowledge that if I gave in to the temptation an inevitable sequence of events would be set in motion. Greed and the prospect of new clothes settled the argument, but I compromised by only stealing from one individual and by not taking all he had. I was twenty pounds richer but walking home that evening I felt somehow different to when I'd set out that morning.

In the club that night, wearing new trousers and jacket, I started talking to a dark skinny lad who was just as drunk as me. He had just been released from Dartmoor and we took turns expressing the anger we felt for the bastards who locked us up. By the time the club closed we were both in the mood for getting our own back with some burglary on our way home. The tried and tested method of kicking in the glass door got us inside a high-street store and we left through the back weighed down with sheepskin coats, jeans and shirts. Half a mile down the road a car pulled up, four men got out and moved towards us in the orchestrated fashion of police officers. I sobered up immediately as the familiar gut-wrenching fear swept over me. It always came at the moment of arrest but passed as I adjusted to the experience of being locked up. This time however arrest felt much worse. I knew I had well and truly screwed up everything.

It was past four in the morning. I'd made a statement and was sitting on the wooden bench in the underground police cell unable to escape into sleep. This time mum an dad were sure to wash their hands of me. I was on my own again and the only security facing me was the familiarity of prison life, eighteen months of it at least. I couldn't understand why I wasn't taken in front of the magistrates. I'd been staring at the graffiti on the cell wall for hours. Perhaps there would be a court sitting in the afternoon? A policeman unlocked the door and passed through a paper plate with chips and ham but I wasn't hungry. He came back an hour later and said, 'Right, time your was off home.' There was always one who had to kick you when you were down, I thought. Very funny. Big joke. I followed him upstairs and into an office where a sergeant told me that as a result of the recent new criminal justice act I was being released on bail to appear in court at some later date. It took a while to sink in. I didn't believe what I'd heard until I was standing on the street outside, confused. I was pleased to be out of the cell but I had no idea if I could go home to mum and dad. If I did, what would I say?

But the house at Pennycross was empty. Dad was at work and mum was probably out shopping. Opening my bedroom door I saw all my clothes neatly folded as if to be packed away. My other possessions had been put in a cardboard box. It didn't feel like my room and it seemed obvious I wasn't wanted there anymore. I was just about to leave the house when mum walked in. She threw her arms round me and, before I had time to think, the lie was past my lips. 'The police made a mistake. It was someone else they wanted and they let me go.' I saw the relief on mum's face and followed her into the kitchen where she sat me down and fussed around with the kettle as she spoke about how awful it all must have been for me. It was the same with the rest of the family as they listened and sympathized. By evening any opportunity for truth had passed.

A month passed and still no letter came from the court to tell me when I should appear. The tension of keeping the truth from mum and dad was growing unbearable and I knew I had to run away. It was Friday, wages were due. I would leave work at lunchtime, go home, pack some clothes and get on a train to somewhere far away.

As I painted that day I kept thinking about what I was going to do. When the foreman came round with my wages I had to rub away the tears from my face. I'd been crying all morning but I explained I had a heavy cold. I was about to leave my mum, the most loving person I'd ever known, without even saying goodbye and I felt terrible. There was no point continuing work so I left the paint and the unfinished walls, locked up the house and walked back to Pennycross. I stopped on the way to buy mum the best box of chocolates in the shop. It wasn't much of a gesture but I needed her to know that despite what I was about to do, I loved her. I wished with all my heart she would understand how afraid I was feeling.

Sasha lay quietly on the floor of my bedroom as I packed my clothes, as if she knew it was the last time she'd see me. Mum, dad and the family were already a part of my past. I packed away some of Anthony's clothes. Mum wouldn't be doing any more of my laundry so I took the iron as well. Downstairs in the kitchen I forced open the electric meter and tipped out onto the table a heap of silver fifty pence pieces which I guessed amounted to about fifty pounds. As I wrapped them in one of mum's tea towels, I shivered. I knew then there was no going back.

As if on cue I heard the sound of a car horn. The taxi I had phoned earlier was waiting outside. I stood for a moment in the only real home I'd ever had to feel for the last time the presence of the love I'd been given. In the hall I sank to my knees and kissed Sasha goodbye and ruffled Merlin's hair. I remembered another red setter from years before and another house with Aunty standing in the hall crying as she waited to say goodbye, and outside that house another car waiting to take me away forever. The taxi driver sounded the horn a second time and I knew it was time to leave. I can't remember closing the front door behind me. The next thing which registered was sitting on a train travelling towards Manchester.

I was evil. The knowledge of what I was capable of had always been lurking deep inside me but now it was out in the open. I drank steadily in the train's buffet compartment but the alcohol did nothing to dilute the filth I felt inside of me. As soon as I got to Manchester I made for the nearest gay pub and continued drinking but it was impossible to hide from what I'd done. I had been stealing all of my life but this time it was different and what I'd done felt like it was killing me. I had no future – I'd left that behind in Pennycross. I knew it was only a matter of time before I went back into prison and I didn't care where or when it happened.

A boy from my younger days in London was in the pub. Charlie had been in great demand as a prostitute but had eventually come back to his home in Manchester. He invited me back to his flat for the night and I went with him, grateful for any kind of company. We drank, smoked hash and had sex in his bed made up on the floor but afterwards I still couldn't sleep. I got up and walked naked to the bathroom to drink some cold water, leaving Charlie sleeping peacefully. I switched on the bathroom light and saw a squat brown bottle labelled Mogadon sitting on the side of the bath. The untidy pile of white pills inside glowed yellow in the fluorescent glare of the overhead tube. There was nothing else in the room but the bottle. It seemed to beckon me towards it, the pills inside calling like sinister friends, whispering in the dead of night that every event in my life had been part of a conspiracy to lead us to this meeting. I was exhausted, beaten, had nowhere else to go.

But I didn't want to die in Charlie's flat. I was the one to be punished, not him. When I left Charlie's flat in the morning I'd take the bottle with me. I went back and laid on the bed and I knew I would finally be able to sleep. When I woke Charlie was up cooking breakfast. I dressed and went to the bathroom and, although I searched every-where, the small brown bottle had gone.

I spent the next month in Manchester breaking into houses near the area where I'd once lived with Chris. I rented a cheap bedsit and it was there early one morning that the police caught up with me. I didn't care. I wasn't even relieved. The police station was exactly as I remem-bered it and the detective constable was the same one who had arrested me the last time. Unlike a lot of policemen I'd known, he didn't try to use psychology to get me to tell the truth – I would have told it to anyone. Before locking me back in the cell he asked if there was anything he could get me. Without thinking I asked for a watch. He said he'd see what he could do and, before closing the door, said, 'Despite what you think you're not the normal sort of criminal I come across.'

Risley remand centre was even dirtier and more barren than when I'd known it. In those days the cell windows had glass; now they were covered with bits of cardboard or scraps of blanket. There was the predictable wait of several weeks before I appeared in front of the Judge at the Crown Court and no surprise when he sentenced me to four years.

'Not you again!' said the screw on reception duty at Strangeways. It was a phrase repeated many times over the first few days on the wing. On the surface I feigned a couldn't-care-less attitude but inside I was full of regrets for what I'd done to mum and dad.

As on my first stay in Strangeways I soon had a taste of solitary confinement down the block. It was a different chaplain who made the daily visit and this time I was always eager for him to stay and talk. One bleak morning he spoke directly about Jesus. Considering myself quite an authority on things religious, I said I couldn't believe in such a character and went on to add that if he did exist and he could take away the pain I'd caused mum, then I would believe in him. The chaplain listened attentively as I recounted the events in Plymouth. He spoke about forgiveness but didn't seem to understand I was past caring about myself and only wanted to repair the damage I'd done to the family who had made me their own.

Back on the main wing the general topic of conversation was the acquittal of Jeremy Thorpe, then leader of the Liberal Party, on a charge of conspiracy to murder. There was also a letter for me from the Inland Revenue and a cheque for £180. Some weeks previously I'd applied for a tax rebate and as soon as the cheque cleared I intended to send back to mum what I'd stolen from the meter. To complete the day I was informed by the allocation screw I'd be transferred shortly to Lancaster.

Only the inmates' faces had changed at Lancaster. There were none of the derisive comments which greeted me at Strangeways – quite the reverse in fact. Greetings like 'How's it going Willy?' from the screws who remembered me and Phyllis the probation officer set up our weekly meetings again which helped lighten the burden of Plymouth. I was a known quantity, not a security risk and very soon back outside working on the farm. In a way I felt quite at home.

The best thing to happen in the early weeks was a letter from mum. She said how pleased she had been to hear from me and how much pleasure it had given her to receive the money I'd sent and to know I wasn't that bad. Despite the warmth of her letter and assurance of forgiveness, I was still aware I had trampled over something very precious and which could never be quite the same again.

The one major difference on my return to Lancaster was my lack of success in picking up young men. Whenever the prison coach carrying new receptions came through the main gates I'd closely scrutinize the passengers. There might be one or two that took my fancy, but my old methods of scoring just weren't working anymore. I felt older and more unattractive than I'd ever done before. I blamed the prison. With just two hundred inmates the options were limited – I needed to be in a larger prison if things were to improve. With the excuse that I needed escape from past associations and complete my sentence in a different environment, I applied for a transfer which I immediately regretted on being told I was to go to Preston prison.

The regime there was a world apart from Lancaster with discipline akin to that in Strangeways. On my first night I was banged up with a meth-drinking dosser who was lying on his bed in a sea of rotting food which littered the cell floor. I put up with the stench for one night then asked the landing screw for a cell change. The prison was full to the brim – there wasn't another space available anywhere. Furious I pointed out the conditions I'd been forced to sleep in the night before. The screw apologized and said I'd just have to put up with it for a few days. I marched back to the cell, packed my few belongings into a blanket and stood outside on the landing. When the screw came along to bang up the cell door I refused to go inside. He had not choice – I was nicked for disobeying a direct order and taken down the block. The governor was sympathetic but gave me an official caution before issuing instructions that another cell be found.

My negative attitude to the prison began to change as I

found my way around and discovered the thriving gay scene. My hopes were focused on a young boy called Mark who worked in the prison shirt tailoring shop. He was small, cute and fully aware that he was in demand. With no confidence in my own appeal I kept my distance but I knew he'd noticed my interest .

I was assigned the job of locations orderly, and with this came the privilege of a red armband. The prison had a population of more than four hundred short-term prisoners of its own as well as taking the overspill from Manchester, Leeds and Liverpool. With such a high turnover of receptions and discharges the screws needed a central reference point to discover where inmates physically were should they be needed for a visit or any other reason . So my responsibility was to keep a daily record in three giant ledgers of each inmate's name, sentence, cell location and place of work. The red band on my arm was the authority I needed to walk freely round the prison and to ask for any locked gate barring my passage to be opened. This status was the key to getting closer to Mark.

With six months left to serve, I was selected for one of the limited places on the prison's pre-release hostel scheme designed to help inmates readjust to the outside world by spending the tail-end of their sentence in full-time employment, hence, in theory, earning enough money to carry them through the early days of release. The hostel was a small residential building set inside the prison. The men living there were allowed out during the day to visit the job centre or to chase positions advertised in the local paper. When employment was found a deduction was taken from their wages to cover board and lodging, a small proportion given back for pocket money and the remainder banked by the hostel warden and then returned on the inmate's release. After a month in residence the inmate was allowed to spend the weekend with family, if he had any, and on weekday evenings he was free to leave the prison as long as he returned by ten o'clock. I learnt of my selection for the scheme in September and had six weeks left to wait before a place became vacant.

Walking freely about the prison as locations orderly I began chatting to a West Indian boy in his twenties who I met on one of the wings. I didn't find him physically attractive but we shared a facility for speaking in exaggerated home counties accents. He wore horn-rimmed glasses perched on the nose of his finely chiselled ebony face and seemed very impressed with my apparent knowledge of spiritual matters. Outside he was a compulsive gambler and to finance his habit he had resorted to theft which had resulted in more than one prison sentence. I had tired of Buddhism and had begun moving back towards Christianity and when I first met Ruel he had just become interested in the bible. I was constantly surprised at the way authoritative sermons to him spewed spontaneously out of my mouth. I could tell he was impressed by the confident way I expressed the need for salvation through embracing Jesus Christ as his Lord and Master. I was thrilled when he confessed how at four in the morning he had risen from the bed in his cell, knelt on the floor and prayed for Jesus to come into his life: I had made my first convert. Ruel treated me as his spiritual master and heaped praise and gratitude on me for showing him the true path. I could see a whole new future opening up for me too, as an evangelist whose audiences would rival those who flocked to see the likes of Billy Graham.

Most of the material I had used on my sermons to Ruel had been gleaned from evangelical books I took from the prison library. A lot of them were autobiographical works detailing depraved lives which had been transformed by Jesus. After reading several I began to believe I could look to a future in which God had a special plan for me – this would not of course include stealing or prison sentences. Ruel was released a week before I joined the hostel scheme and went to live at a Christian-run hostel in Manchester. He spoke about the part I had played in his conversion and a letter came extending an invitation to join him there when I got out. I was transferred to the hostel before the official date because the education department made arrangements for me to take up a course at an outside college on criminology. I had expressed an interest in the subject and didn't want to miss the first lesson.

It was like taking part in a dream. One moment I was rushing round the prison keeping ledger books up to date, the next I was dressed in civilian clothes standing at the bus stop on my way to the nearby college. A born-again Christian from Preston had been writing to me for a few weeks so, before the lecture began, I called him to let him know I was out. We hadn't met and at his suggestion we agreed that he would drive me back to the prison after the lecture.

The bulk of the class was made up of middle-aged house-wives who collectively expressed a wish to work with juvenile delinquents. Apart from this group there were two police officers, a doctor and a young couple and I guessed had registered in order to camouflage an illicit affair. The Christian was waiting for me in the college car park afterwards. He was fat, bald and wore sinister dark glasses. I held out my hand for him to shake and he ignored it in favour of throwing his arms around me in an embrace. 'Praise the Lord,' he repeated over and again. He parked the car outside a pub which stood across the road from the prison and continued with his monologue on how great God had been to free me from the prison. I sat pretending to listen but my attention was drawn to the sound of music and laughter from the direction of the pub.

Inwardly I was cursing myself – valuable minutes of my

first taste of freedom were being wasted. I would have much preferred to be drinking my first pint of beer after two years of nothing more stimulating than pint mugs of the prison tea we referred to as 'diesel'.

As it was the responsibility of hostel residents to secure employment I visited the local job centre. With the recession felt worst in the North of England I knew I'd be fortunate to find any work. I tried everywhere without success for a week and on the Sunday went to the church in Preston because there was nothing better to do. When the service finished the vicar shook hands as I filed out with the rest of the congregation and asked if I'd recently moved to the area. I explained in a few quiet words that I'd just been released from prison. He became very interested and invited me to his house for tea the following evening. A dapper little man living in quite opulent surroundings, I told him over cream cakes about myself and the difficulty of finding a job. He asked if I had any skills so I told him about the work I had done as decorator. He excused himself for a moment and crossed his study to the phone. When he sat back down I had a job to start the next day with a parishioner who owned a painting contractor's firm in the town.

Everything seemed to be working out. The foreman of the painting firm was satisfied with my work and I was looking forward to my first full weekend away from the hostel staying with Ruel at the Beeches hostel in Manchester. I was with a gang painting a shop in Burnley that day but an hour later I was on my way back to Preston. A jacket in the window display of the shop had taken my fancy and someone had seen me as I hid it. The hostel warden was waiting at the firm's office with the proprietor. I strenuously denied any connection with the theft and accused the only witness of being the thief himself. It was my word against his but I was given my cards and driven back to the prison. The hostel warden was very supportive and not only believed my side of the story but said so to the governor when I was called up to see him.

I spent that Christmas with Ruel at the Beeches. During the holiday season I'd spent a lot of time thinking about Mark, the boy who worked in the prison sewing-machine shop. I knew Christmas hadn't been much fun for him. I'd written to him several times and had sent him a watch and radio. He lived in Manchester and I was hoping to get together with him when he got out. On my next evening out in Preston I had a few pints of beer and smuggled a quarter bottle of whisky back into the hostel concealed down my underpants – I wanted to surprise Mark who was in a cell on the ground floor. The front door of the hostel was routinely locked at ten o'clock but by using the fire door key I slipped out through the back entrance and into the main prison grounds. In the dark, my mind fuddled with beer, I couldn't find Mark's cell. After a while I gave up and made my way back to the hostel. I was nearly there when a patrolling screw came round the corner and almost bumped into me. He was an elderly auxiliary officer and he jumped with fright at discovering someone at large in the prison grounds. 'Don't worry,' I said, 'I'm from the hostel. I didn't feel well and needed some fresh air.' His voice was still shaking as he told me I'd better get back there, quick. Ten minutes later a posse of screws arrived at the hostel and escorted me into the sleeping prison where they locked me in the block. The prison grapevine, efficient as ever, brought me a message from Mark the next morning to say I was a fool. The governor agreed, adding I'd spend the remainder of my sentence where I was.

CHAPTER 14

BEING RELEASED FROM PRISON ALWAYS SEEMED TO HAPPEN around the Easter period. It was the same getting out of Preston. I went to stay with Ruel and the other people living at the Beeches, a large house converted into a collection of bedsits and small flats. Half of the residents were young, rather vapid, born-again Christians. The others mostly boys under twenty placed there by the social services or prison after-care departments. The hostel had been set up and subsidized by a charity which aimed to provide residents they deemed in need with a support network and desirable influences.

Ruel had changed beyond all recognition – he was one of the Christians, the most popular of all. I was enormously impressed by the integrity which characterized his new life-style. His days began with the bible and prayers and from then on he was kept busy visiting people in hospital or listening to people in need. On moving into the hostel I tried to emulate the sincerity of Ruel's faith, but I knew I was kidding myself. I found the company of the other Christians boring and irritating. There didn't seem to be an individual voice amongst them. The only time they ever became animated and expressed any emotion was at their prayer groups. I much preferred the company of the youngsters. They were pretty sceptical about the motives of the Christians and let their feelings be known to me. Ruel escaped any criticism: he'd been there himself. He smiled and talked with them without being judgemental or patronizing. At times I even felt envious of what he'd become: the pupil had outgrown his teacher.

The assistant warden of the hostel, Simon, was the son of a priest and I'd first met him in the chaplain's group at Lancaster prison where he was serving his first sentence after getting involved with some tearaways planning to carry out a robbery. Their bravado got them all nicked. Simon was supposed to be a get-away driver, but fell asleep at the wheel and was arrested when a patrolling policeman searched the boot of his car and discovered the tools of the trade for a hold up. In his mid-twenties, Simon was a big strong lad who spent a lot of his time working out in the gym and at weekends he had a job as a night club bouncer. I knew Simon was in a similar situation to me, but for him it was even more difficult. In the prison he'd been absorbed with being a Christian so much that he was offered the position of assistant warden at the Beeches. He was supposed to be both an example of what God could do and a man with knowledge of living on the other side. At prayer meetings I'd open my eyes and look round at the fervent expressions on the Christians' faces but Simon's face registered nothing but boredom. When prayers were over we'd decline the tea and biscuits and drive his van to Moss Side for some music, drugs and life. The youngsters in the hostel were all fond of Simon. He had a way of relating to them like a big friendly brother. I didn't take much notice at first but gradually his popularity began getting under my skin too.

I discovered during a conversation with one of the youngsters that Simon had been responsible for the theft of a social security giro which had been sent addressed to a lad who had since left. Simon had got the boy I was talking with to cash the giro at the post office and split the proceeds between them. I was furious. How dare he involve the youngster in crime? He had no right to the position he held and his influence with the kids. I went to Ruel's room and beat around the bush to stoke up his curiosity before recounting the story I'd been told. I sat with him for hours as he agonized over what he should do. Simon was his friend – he didn't want to judge or inform. He leafed through his bible searching for some precedent or guidance on how to act. In between the pauses I subtly added fuel to the suggestion that the hostel's trustees be told.

I agreed to accompany Ruel when he did the deed. I kept my face as long and as serious as his. I nodded in agreement as Ruel explained how unpleasant it was to bring such unpleasant news about his friend. But by the time we got back to the Beeches, we knew that Simon was to be sacked.

Simon's departure from the Beeches created an atmosphere of instability. The Christians were embarrassed at his fall from grace, the youngsters resentful that he'd been pushed out. I didn't feel too good about how I'd betrayed him and disrupted what had once been a congenial place. I went to work on the Saturday evening relieved to leave the mess behind me for a few hours. I was working nights behind a hotel reception desk. At midnight I started drinking large whiskies from the residents' bar. After it closed and the residents and staff were in bed, I started on the vodka. Later that morning I felt I had to get away from Manchester and the Beeches. The ideal place to hide would be London. A phone call established that the first train left Manchester at 6.30, which gave me enough time to open the hotel safe and add the money I stole from there to the bar takings. Six hundred pounds: enough to find a room, a job and a new start in the capital.

I rented a top floor bedsit close to Queen's Park Rangers football ground. The first night I was woken by voices shouting excitedly in the back garden below. From the window I looked down on jumping torch beams illuminating the silver buttons on police uniforms. There were at least a dozen of them and I thought how have they got on to me so fast? But it wasn't me they were after. There was a sudden surge of movement and they leapt over garden fences after a lone figure a few yards ahead of them. Back in the narrow bed with the lump mattress I wondered how long it would be before I would have to start running again. A few days later, a West End job centre sent me to a theatrical supply shop in Drury Lane. It was a filthy job where I spent my day in a small basement filled with drums of various powders which were mixed with water to make the paint for stage scenery. Orders were shouted down from the serving area of the shop above. 'A kilo of puce. Half a vermilion.' It went on all day and by the time I went home the powder from the drums was in the pores of my skin, clogging my nose and distorting the colour of my clothes. I could have caught a bus or taken the tube home but usually I walked along Oxford Street, past Hyde Park and from Bayswater into Hammersmith. The journey took an hour and a half. I wasn't hurrying. I searched the faces in the crowds thronging the busy streets hoping I might catch sight of Chris. I'd heard from a mutual acquaintance that he had his own house and was doing well in his profession. I lived in a dingy bedsit, my evening meal came from the cheap end of the chip shop and I counted myself lucky if I could afford a couple of cans of drink to knock me out to sleep. At the time it had been hell living with Chris but now if I'd seen him on the street I would have said I was sorry and hoped once again he'd rescue me from the mess my life was in.

My vigilance did spot one face from the past. Peter was a

good looking straight guy of mixed race I'd first met on the Dilly where, like me, he was looking for a punter. He was four years younger than me and had similar experience of life in children's homes. Most of the time we spent together was in the regular periods of estrangement from his girlfriend Jackie. She was related to a singer from a famous rock group and when they asked if I would be best man at their wedding I felt I'd inched my way a bit further towards fame.

I hadn't seen Peter in almost ten years. He was still very handsome but there was an expression of tiredness masking his face. He was as pleased as I was to make contact with the past and suggested we go for a drink just off Oxford Street. He wasn't with Jackie anymore and saw little of his baby daughter who had been fostered. His love for Jackie had soured into hatred but they had met in the same children's home and without her Peter was lost. Now he was living in a small flat in Victoria with a Spanish waiter who cooked his meals, washed his socks and gave him a little pocket money. We were both in the same position: trapped.

I began to feel distinctly uncomfortable when Peter asked if I had the bottle to work with him on an armed robbery. I asked him a lot of questions, hoping to point out the high risks of such a venture, but he swept my objections aside. For the rest of the evening he talked of nothing but shotguns and I began to suspect he was capable of more than just robbery.

The conditions and pay at the theatrical supply shop were so poor I looked for another job. This time the employment centre directed me to a thermal underwear shop in the West End. The manageress who interviewed me for the vacancy of storeman was large, middle-aged and maternal. She reminded me very much of Phyllis, my probation officer friend from Lancaster. It was easy to smile and be charming because I felt I knew the lady sitting behind her desk. There were other applicants but I knew she liked me when she began going into great detail about what the job entailed. The last thing she came to was the storeman's responsibility to bank each day's takings and suddenly I didn't want the job. I only had one outstanding offence against me, in Manchester. I thought if I stayed out of trouble for a few years it would keep me from prison if I was ever arrested. I explained to the manageress how I'd once spent some time in prison. There didn't seem a need to say how many times. I said I thought she should know and that because of the banking duties would choose someone else. She seemed very impressed by my openness and shook hands saying she might be in touch. The next day, a letter arrived offering me the job.

Working in the West End gave me a chance to investigate the possibility of tracking down my father. The Nigerian Embassy was a short walk from the thermal underwear shop so, one lunch-break, I walked into reception. The girl behind the desk was helpful when I said why I'd come and directed me into another part of the Embassy. A chubby black African, his face marked by tribal scars, sat behind a desk in a charcoal grey suit. He didn't seem particularly interested in why I was there and, because I wasn't sure of pronouncing what I believed was my father's name correctly, I wrote it down on a piece of paper and handed it to him. There was an abrupt change in his attitude. He'd recognized the name. I thought this was the point where he would run off to fetch the Ambassador and when limousines would finally move into my life in a big way.

'Are you sure!' asked the African. I said as best I can be. I could see he needed time to think and he asked if I would call back the next day. He was all smiles when I returned and said that my situation was one of great delicacy due to the position my father held in African society. The solution was to leave it entirely in his hands – the fewer that knew the better. It just so happened, he said, that he would be travelling to Lagos in two weeks and would take steps to contact my father personally. I began relating to the African quite naturally as the first of many loyal servants. The feeling of rank was quite subtle but quite correct for the son of a chief. It was time for me to get back to the underwear shop but the African was loath to let me go. Before leaving his office I agreed to meet him on the steps of the Embassy after work. He wanted to see where I lived and to pick up any photos I had of myself.

The African was waiting outside the Embassy and I assumed we would be ushered into the back of an official car. Instead we travelled to my place on the top deck of a London bus. It took for ever to get to Hammersmith through the thick rush hour traffic and my initial favourable impression of the African was rapidly deteriorating. When I let him into my bed-sit and sat him on the only chair he asked if I usually had visitors. I was expecting Peter and more talk of shotguns but I didn't tell the African this. He wanted to know if I lived with anyone, had any close women friends. From past experience I recognized the tone in his voice which scouts ahead of seduction. He had just passed the point of telling me how good looking I was and how in Nigeria sex between men wasn't frowned on when Peter knocked on the door. I introduced him to the African who made excuses about having to leave and get home to his wife. He didn't ask for any photos before going and it dawned on me then he was little more than an Embassy filing clerk pursuing an agenda of his own. I was annoyed at being taken in, for believing that my father would provide for me a new life. I wouldn't be visiting the Embassy again.

On my thirty-first birthday a man came into the underwear shop and collapsed. The first sign that something was wrong was a chorus of alarm from the female staff behind the counter. I heard one of the staff call me in a voice which cracked on the edge of hysteria and rushing out to the front of the shop I saw the crumpled body of the old man lying on the floor. I could feel myself shaking. No one in the shop seemed able to move and for a moment we were stuck in a tableau. I'd worked in hospitals so I knelt down beside the fallen figure and felt for a pulse in his wrist. I wasn't sure if there was one or even if my finger was in the right place. I didn't know what to do next. The old man's face was a blue grey colour. Tiny white bubbles of froth appeared on his lips and began to dribble down his chin. I still had the old man's wrist in my hand and was just about to place him in a more comfortable position when I had the distinct impression that he wasn't there anymore but was hovering above near the ceiling looking down. I whispered that I thought he was dead. One of the staff who had settled down a bit spoke quietly to the old man's wife and took her into the staff room for a cup of sweet tea. I took on the responsibility of clearing the shop of bystanders. Some of the customers complained but the staff relieved with something to do ushered them out onto the street. I performed heart massage as best I could and when the ambulance staff arrived they asked me to continue. An oxygen mask was strapped to the old man's face and he was hurriedly lifted onto a stretcher. As he was carried to the door and placed in the ambulance I kept on working. I would have liked to have gone with him to the hospital. For the first time in my life I felt quite useful. A few days later a letter arrived from the old man's daughter thanking the staff warmly for the sensitive way her mother had been treated and for the efforts made on her father's behalf before he died.

The old man's death was a cathartic experience. I was

getting older – I couldn't spend the rest of my life unpacking women's underwear. Peter, who had taken to calling at the shop each lunchtime, was waiting for the day I would disappear with the takings. I'd mentioned it as a possibility for financing the purchase of the gun he kept going on about. A few days after the old man's death he turned up as usual. A big smile crossed his face when I said let's do it. I'd arranged to bank the previous day's takings during my lunch hour to give me that little extra time when I wasn't expected back. I knew that by stealing the cash I was on my way back to prison but life was short and I wanted to enjoy some of it then. There was more than a thousand pounds in cash which I transferred to my pockets – the cheques and credit card vouchers I placed in an envelope and posted back to the shop.

Peter wanted to start an immediate search for a gun but, still not enthused by his plans, I insisted on a night out in Manchester. From Heathrow we could be there in forty minutes and in plenty of time to hit the pubs and clubs. The trip was a disappointment. It was the beginning of the week, raining, and hardly anyone out on the town. Afterwards, a young smooth-skinned rent boy agreed to come back to my five-star hotel room. His repertoire of services wasn't very imaginative and for forty pounds I had the frustrating pleasure of watching him strip naked and wank himself off. He said a repeat performance would only cost another twenty pounds.

The streets and shops of London were bright with Christmas decorations. With the festive season less than a week away it was impossible to ignore all the traditional signs of approaching celebration. I felt terrible. The money I'd stolen from Damart's was almost gone, I was living in a seedy bed-and-breakfast hotel in Earl's Court and Peter was out looking for a shotgun. I could feel my life spinning out of control again, heading down a track towards certain destruction. Peter scared me. He was deadly serious about doing an armed robbery and he had my complicit agreement to join him. Sitting in a gay bar which had been commandeered by a boozing and giggling office party crowd I thought about the previous few months and chastized myself for being such an impulsive fool. If I hadn't acted so deviously at the Beeches in getting Simon sacked I wouldn't be sitting where I was now. I had no real friends in London, Peter was trying to destroy me and there was nowhere left to run. Until then, I had only two outstanding offences against me which might not necessarily mean an automatic further prison sentence. If I gave myself up to the police I could halt the merry-go-round of crime I was getting caught up in once again.

Peter still hadn't found the weapon he was looking for so I told him I knew a man I could see and took back the two hundred pounds I'd given him. I left him sitting in the pub, promising to return in a couple of hours and caught a taxi to Euston station. Back in Manchester I phoned Ruel at the Beeches and explained I was handing myself in for the hotel job I'd pulled. (The police had come looking for me at the hostel and Ruel was familiar with the details.) He wanted to come with me to lend moral support and suggested I meet him at the Hostel. Ever optimistic, Ruel assumed that I'd returned to the Christian fold and was seeking to make amends. I went along with the fiction of the prodigal son's return and quickly began believing it myself. I wanted to give myself up to the Detective Constable who had said I wasn't like a real criminal. I thought he would understand how rapidly everything had gone out of control. He was at the police station when I phoned and with Ruel standing next to me I said I was coming in. He wasn't a bit surprised. 'I thought I'd be hearing from you,' he said. I apologized for stealing from the hotel – it was part of his patch and he'd called in one Saturday evening while I was working behind the reception desk. I remembered how he'd told me to keep my nose clean because the hotel owners were friends of his and by rights he should have alerted them about having unknowingly employed a persistent thief. He was sorry I had messed up so quickly after leaving prison but if I wanted to give myself up I should leave it until the New Year – there was no point me being locked up over Christmas. The unexpected reprieve was a relief but it left me with a financial problem. I was so sure this was my last day of freedom that I'd spent the remainder of my money on a radio, a watch, a ring and a gold chain with a crucifix. These were the items a prisoner was allowed to possess inside and which for me would have been a comfort as status symbols.

I hoped that I might be able to stay at the Beeches but the Christians weren't at all keen. They thought I'd be a bad influence on the younger residents. As a compromise a collection was made which was enough for me to pay a week's board in advance at the YMCA. Ruel came over to visit most days. He introduced me to a circle of born-again Christians based in the city centre and I went to communion every morning at the local church. The parish priest invited me to lunch and was impressed when I told him I'd found my way back to God and that the price I might have to pay was going to prison. I made an appointment with a solicitor and gave him the same reason why I was giving myself up. He was far more sceptical and suggested a psychiatrist's report might help in mitigation when I appeared in court. I left his office offended. The solicitor was implying I was mad – he didn't understand I'd had a change of heart and was beginning a new life led by the Lord. I felt more positively towards him when at the first court hearing he persuaded the magistrates to grant me bail on my own surety. I was even more encouraged by his opinion he could probably get met off with a probation order. My new Christian life seemed to be paying dividends.

Randall, one of the city-centre Christians believed the panacea for all spiritual ills was baptism. He accepted I'd repented of my former life but insisted that the pact I had made with God still needed to be sealed. One afternoon early in January I called to see Randall at the meeting centre he ran and told him of a vivid dream I'd had the night before in which both of my feet had become leprous. They were covered in weeping sores and my toes were rotting away. He needed no further evidence – it was vital I be baptised that very day. A telephone call was made to the Beeches summoning Ruel and whoever else wanted to witness the ceremony. The centre was closed and Randall went to fetch his transit van from the car park. He was like an excited child looking forward to a great treat. There were eight of us in the van as it travelled out of Manchester. Randall, a giant bear of a man with a wild and full tangled beard, said he knew of a river in Cheshire and put his foot down on the accelerator.

We had to cross a couple of muddy fields to get to the place Randall was leading us to. I didn't want to leave the van. It was a cold day in Manchester but out in the country it was perishing. There was worse to come. Randall believed in nothing less than total immersion for the efficacy of baptism. It was too late to back out but it still didn't seem quite right. When we reached the river Randall waded out with his trouser legs rolled up and stopped where the depth of the water reached his knees. The other Christians stood shivering on the bank and watched as I undressed down to just jeans and a tee shirt. One of the Christians carried the bag which held some towels. Another had a flask of hot soup. It's going to take more than that to warm me up I thought as I gritted my teeth against the icy water round my legs and moved towards Randall who seemed oblivious of the cold as he prayed out loud.

He continued praying as he supported me from behind and lowered me backwards and under the freezing water. I felt the initial shock of being completely submerged in the chill river and then I was standing back up on my feet again as Randall flung his arms around me calling out, 'Praise the Lord. God is good. Praise the Lord.' I could see his lips moving and hear the words, but Randall seemed as insubstantial as celluloid. I looked towards the bank where the other Christians were standing and it was the same – they weren't real, they were images on a distant cinema screen. I wasn't aware of the cold. I couldn't feel the arms which were placed round me by each Christian in turn. I dried myself mechanically with the towels which were handed me and got changed into some old clothes of Randall's with the fumbling you'd expect from a child attempting to tie his shoelaces for the first time. A large section of my mind had ceased to function. I'd felt like this before but only on LSD. I said nothing on the journey back to Manchester. I wanted to sleep. It wasn't much but I wanted to get back to the safety of my little room at the YMCA.

This detached, almost hallucinogenic condition, with my rational capacity replaced by cotton wool and thick burnt rubber, lasted for several days. I stayed in my room for much of the time and then one afternoon I was walking gingerly down the stairs, holding tight to the bannister when everything suddenly went haywire. There was a loud whirring in my head like the sound of a tape on fast wind. It raced so fast but the machine was my mind and who I was. Like an engine being revved too high there was nothing I could do but cling to the bannister rail and hope the craziness would stop. It did, just as suddenly as it began, as if I'd just woken out of a nightmare. The first thought I'd had for days was, 'What the fuck are you doing here in Manchester playing the born-again Christian? I'm going back to London.'

My social security giro was due and as soon as I'd cashed it I went to the city centre and found the shop I'd seen advertised as specializing in imitation firearms. For twenty-five pounds I purchased a mean looking handgun which would be more than adequate for scaring people in the robberies I intended carrying out. Some sleight of hand on a car sales forecourt provided me with a set of ignition keys. Forty minutes later I was driving on the motorway towards London in an orange Morris Marina and on the seat beside me was a bottle of whisky to swig from. I felt alive for the first time in ages. I saw myself as a solider declaring a one-man war on the world. My enemies would be the police and, outnumbered as I was, the battle would probably mean my death. I didn't care. I would snarl even as the police bullets smashed through my brain. Rather that than the life of a wimp holy Joe!

CHAPTER 15

LONDON WAS COLD, DAMP AND WRAPPED IN A THICK GREY evening fog. I parked the car in a quiet side street near the New King's Road in Fulham. From where I sat in the car I could see the bottle-filled shelves of the off-licence I was about to rob. I hadn't given any thought as to where I'd pull my first job. I'd just instinctively steered the car to an area I was familiar with. I adjusted the heavy scarf around my neck and the lower part of my face, confident that my muffled appearance would be in keeping with the unpleasant weather conditions. I checked a couple of times that the gun would slip easily from my pocket and left the car with the driver's door slightly open.

A bell rang loudly as I pushed open the off-licence door. There was only one person behind the counter – a pleasant faced young man in his late twenties. He looked up and smiled in a helpful way and asked if I wanted the cheap bottle of wine I'd selected from the special offer display wrapped or in a bag. I handed him my last five pound note and as he looked down towards the till and was picking out my change I pulled the gun from my pocket and pointed it at his head. He looked up from the till and for an instant, before registering he was staring down the barrel of a gun, his lips moved towards a practised smile which died and became a frightened squeal of alarm as he backed away against the shelves behind him. As I reached over the counter transferring notes from the till into my pocket another young man appeared from the rear of the premises. He must have heard his colleague cry out and it looked as though he was intent on moving to the front door to summon assistance. 'Get back or I'll blow your fucking head off!' I warned. He did as he was ordered. 'Now you too,' I growled at the first assistant, 'round the back and if you want a bullet in your head poke it out of the front door in the next two minutes.' I picked up the bottle of wine the assistant had wrapped for me and casually left the shop. Driving in the direction of Earl's Court I passed sirens and blue lights racing to the scene I'd just left.

I felt great. It had been so easy – all you needed was some bottle and you were invincible. I'd crossed an invisible barrier that set me apart from ordinary people. At last I'd come out of hiding and had taken what I wanted by threatening violence. With a make-believe gun in my hand I'd had my first taste of real power. From now on I was going to start enjoying life. With money in my pocket there would be no shortage of boys. The lean days were over and I was on my way to the Boltons for my first night of fun.

The Boltons had been one of my favourite haunts during my earliest days in London. I didn't expect to see many familiar faces but with a wad of banknotes in my pocket it wasn't long before I was buying drinks for a thin, dark-haired boy from Glasgow. Like many others, John had come to the capital to make money and he wasn't particular how he did it. We went on to a club together and feeling more than a little pleased with myself I hinted I was into pretty heavy stuff as a way of making a living. This prompted John whose tongue had been loosened by drink and speed to regale me with some of the violent methods he'd used to rob punters who thought they would just be paying him for sex. I wasn't sure if he was straight or what but he seemed more than impressed when I admitted to being in a similar line of work. I quite liked the idea of taking him on as my apprentice. I reckoned that whatever his sexual orientation he'd be so pleased with the cash I could put his way and wasn't likely to turn me down sexually. He wasn't living anywhere permanent and was quite happy to share my bed in the hotel I booked into. The off-licence robbery had netted almost three hundred pounds and most of it had gone on my first night on the town. I wasn't worried. There was plenty more where that came from and I promised John before we fell asleep I'd take him on my next job the following evening.

We toured Belgravia in the orange Marina before settling on a small supermarket tucked away in a quiet back street. We didn't have to say a word. The shop was about to close when we walked in together. I pulled the gun from my pocket. The two female assistants froze and John, as if he'd been doing it all his life, walked calmly behind the counter and emptied both tills. We were back at it the next day. This time I chose Wimbledon. From my brief time as a supermarket employee I'd learnt how insurance companies would only be liable for a maximum amount of money held overnight on the premises. The logical deduction was to identify a late night supermarket and waylay whichever member of staff took the day's takings to the night safe. I chose a fairly large shop and sent John in to see if he could spot who was the boss. He reported back with the description of a man wearing a white shirt and glasses. We had to wait around for a while before he appeared but it was obvious where he was going. It was another cold night and he came out of the shop carrying a carrier bag but still dressed only in shirtsleeves. There were still a lot of people on the street but none of them noticed us crowding the guy as he dug in his pocket for the key to the night safe. I had my lines off perfectly. I let him see the gun and promised to blow his fucking head off if he didn't hand over the bag quietly and then walk away in the direction I pointed him to. It was my best job yet: fifteen hundred pounds. Back at the Boltons we joked about being able to take a couple of days off. I'd also decided that shop tills were off the agenda – it was more profitable to concentrate on night safes.

I took an immediate liking to Alex, a Glaswegian lad introduced to me by John. In his late twenties he was too old for me to be interested in sexually but I could still see the traces of an unusually beautiful young boy in his finely chiselled face. John wanted to spend a few days out of London visiting his brother in Jersey. He knew Alex was in the same line of work as us and if I needed some quick cash while he was away Alex would make an ideal partner. He was right. Alex was perfect. We had little to do during the early evening so we robbed an off-licence in Chelsea as a sort of practice run at working together. The harsh brutal Gorbals accent Alex could manufacture was as threatening as the gun in my hand. As if by instinct we worked a variation on the theme of the good and the bad cop. Alex was seen by the victim lying face down on the floor as the one liable to explode into a violent assault while I was the calm reasonable one advising the victim to follow instructions to the letter to avoid unleashing my partner's rage.

By the time John returned from Jersey, Alex and I were close friends. In a few days he'd become almost like a brother. Unlike John who was never very clear about what he liked both Alex and I shared a similar passion for pretty young boys. We went out robbing together and then spent the rest of the night in various gay places, spending heavily and always getting the pick of available boys. We were drawn closer together when I joined him on his heroin habit. He gave me my first hit and forgetting I was new to such a powerful drug injected a similar amount to what he

157

was used to. I didn't remember very much more than everything going black. Alex said later he thought I was going to die but he didn't panic and when I came round a few hours later he was still there.

I was in awe of how confident Alex was each time he met a new boy. I could only charm and impress with the money in my pocket. Most of the boys Alex picked up would have been attracted to him even if he didn't have a penny. His strongest asset (and one I didn't possess at all) was the ability to smile easily. He had a devil-may-care attitude which drew people to him. Alone together even I could laugh with him unself-consciously. I couldn't remember a time when I'd been privileged enough to have such a friend.

John when he returned from Jersey quite naturally assumed he would come back to work with me and for a while we worked three-handed. Not being short of money we paid out a lump sum and moved into a two-bedroomed flat in Knightsbridge. By this time I'd grown tired of John. I was resentful that despite the money I'd helped him make I never had got to bed with him. As far as I was concerned he'd been using me and with Alex on the firm he was really just dead weight. To ease him out I went into retirement for a few days. Both he and Alex had grown used to the arrangement of me making decisions about where we'd hit and as I was the driver and owner of the car they were both dependent on where and when I chose to go out robbing. John's heroin habit was heavy and when his money ran out he stole some from the flat's electric meter. Alex and I agreed this could have meant the police being called by the Irish caretaker which might have exposed us to risk. On this joint agreement we told him to get out. The caretaker was easy to handle. He was an effeminate queen in his sixties who for some reason had never taken to John. We replaced the money he'd taken and gave the caretaker a bottle of whisky for the inconvenience.

I must have been responsible for a dozen or so robberies before I felt the net closing in. Alex and I had been spending money like millionaires for a month. It was obvious from our lifestyle we were up to mischief and anyone listening in to snatches of indiscreet conversation between us wouldn't have had much difficulty in working out what we were up to. One such person became offended one night when Alex chatted up the boy he was with and brought him back to the flat for the night. We were just about to get our heads down when the bell rang and looking out of the window to see who was calling at such a late hour we saw four men at the street door who identified themselves as police and could they come in. Alex and I put on a wonderful act of being harmless queens and looked suitably surprised when one of the coppers said they had received an anonymous phone call to say there was a team of armed robbers living at the address they'd been given. Alex went on to explain the disagreement which had taken place earlier about the boy who had come home with him and this settled their suspicions. It was a close call: a cursory inspection of the flat would have turned up a sizeable assortment of cash bags we'd been too careless to dispose of. The policemen left politely, declining the cup of tea we offered and apologizing for having bothered us at such a late hour. Alex and I both realized it would be best to find somewhere else to live.

We needed some money to finance a move and the most convenient place to rob was a supermarket round the corner from the flat in Sloane Street. We went in just before closing time, herding the four members of staff down into the basement and out of sight of passers by. They were suitably cowed by Alex's aggression and it didn't take me long to empty the safe. To be doubly safe of a smooth getaway I told Alex to keep the shop staff face down on the floor for a minute and then follow me to the car. I had the engine running and the passenger door open ready when he came running round the corner. 'Go! Go! Go!' he shouted, jumping into the car and slamming the passenger door shut. Something had gone wrong – two male members of staff had come after him when he left the shop. As I gunned the car's motor and accelerated away I could see his pursuers just a few yards behind, close enough to be able to read the car's registration plates. We dumped the Marina half a mile further on and made it safely back to the flat by hailing a passing black cab. Now it was imperative that we move from the area.

Without the Marina our options were limited. I thought it best to lie low for a couple of days before venturing out to steal or buy another car. Our stock of heroin was disturbingly low so Alex went out to score while I laid on the living room couch reviewing the previous night's events. Alex reckoned that one of the pursuers had realized we were only carrying imitation guns and that on a busy street there was little danger of physical violence. I wasn't sure. I just was aware we'd had another lucky escape. My nerves were still a bit shot and my heart did a somersault when I heard the doorbell to our flat being rung. It was the Irish caretaker in a state of high excitement. 'The police have just been,' he said. 'They have taken away the two lads who rent the flat upstairs.' The police had told him not to say anything but they were coming back in an hour. 'Something to do with robberies,' he added. I'd seen the upstairs tenants: one was black, the other white. The police had got the wrong flat. I still had time to get out but I was concerned about Alex. He would return with the smack and find the Old Bill waiting for him. I'd never been to the heroin dealer's house but I knew roughly where it was. I just hoped Alex had hung around getting himself a fix. I nearly missed him. I was paying off the driver of the cab which took me to Earl's Court and glanced round at another cab passing on the opposite side of the road. Alex was sat lounging in the back. I screamed out his name and yelled a second time. His head turned and a few yards on the cab pulled into the kerb.

Sitting on the bed of a hotel we booked into and cooking up a fix we talked about what we should do. Our best option it seemed was to get right out of London for a while. All we had between us were the clothes we were dressed in, the gun which I'd shoved in my pocket before leaving the flat and the remaining money from the previous night's robbery. Alex had spent most of his share on a hefty order of smack. One more robbery before we got out would remedy that. We were vulnerable without a car. It would have to be somewhere we could lock the victims in before making our escape. I thought I knew just the place. The off-licence I'd robbed on my first day in London, some six weeks before. We turned up a little before closing time and from the shadow of a doorway across the road I could see there had been a change of staff since my last visit. Our timing was perfect. The shop lights dimmed and the bloke running the place was just placing the key in the door to lock it when we barged in. I did the job for him while Alex pointed the gun and bundled him out of sight into the back office. We left just as smoothly after ripping out the telephone wire and giving the customary warning not to move for two minutes. There was no shortage of cruising cabs. A few minutes later we were back safely in the hotel and five hundred pounds better off.

We didn't get out of bed the next day until early afternoon. Alex wanted to visit his dealer who still had some smack to give him. I said I'd meet him upstairs in the pub where I was going to have lunch. If we were leaving London I'd have to spend less extravagantly for a while: seventy-five pounds for the afternoon should see me through. I tucked the rest of my money away under the carpet and went out. It wasn't a place I used very often but one of the customers with thick silver hair seemed vaguely familiar. He looked up from the table he was sitting at as if expecting some recognition from me but I couldn't place his face. I was just finishing the meal I'd ordered when Alex walked in and threaded his way through the crowd to my table. I was about to ask him what he'd like to drink when we were surrounded by a group of heavily built men. The man with the silver hair leant down to me and said they wanted to talk to us about some armed robberies. 'Have you got anything with you now?' he asked, meaning guns. I said we hadn't and looked at Alex. The blood had drained from his face leaving it white as paper.

The man with the silver hair escorted us discreetly through the lunchtime crowd and asked again, 'You're sure you aren't carrying anything silly?' I felt a slight reduction in the pressure on his grip on the sleeve of my jacket when I said no and that it was only a replica anyway. Outside the pub we had to cross the busy Earl's Court road to where the police had parked their cars. Halfway across the road I remembered where I'd seen silver hair before. He had been with the police who called to the Knightsbridge flat after the anonymous tip off, the one who apologized and politely declined the offer of tea.

As the rear door of the unmarked police car was opened I bent my head and body to slip meekly onto the back seat. At that moment I saw the long years locked inside an image of white tiled institutional walls ahead of me: my life was finished. I didn't want to die in prison, I wanted to be free. Silver hair's grip on my sleeve slackened with my body halfway in the car and as if I'd been taken over by another force I swivelled round, brushed him aside and passed like a ghost through the rest of my captors who stood for a moment as if frozen. I ran like I'd never run before. Behind me I heard a desperate voice cry out, 'Stop him!' I was racing down a one way street against the flow of traffic, so my pursuer's cars were useless. I turned a corner – I was out of sight. Earl's Court tube station had a north and south entrance. I fled down ignoring the official at the barrier and did the same again as I sprinted out onto the street at the other end of the station. I jumped into a taxi which was crawling along the Earl's Court road and with what seemed my last breath gasped, 'Victoria.'

There was a train about to leave for Brighton, as good a place as any. London or Manchester would be too hot for me to hide in. Armed robbery was serious enough, to have escaped from the clutches of the robbery squad compounded the trouble I was in. The police would be furious and would search everywhere for me. When they did get hold of me I'd be due a real kicking. I'd heard all the stories of what took place in the privacy of their cells. I'd always associated police stations with violence. From childhood and Jolliffe in the children's home I'd harboured a terror of being beaten up. It wasn't from any impulse of belated honestly that I willingly signed statements of guilt on arrest, I just didn't want to get battered again. As the train sped towards the coast I tried to imagine what might be happening to Alex. I was afraid for him and felt my escape as a kind of betrayal. If I wasn't such a coward I would give myself up instead of leaving him to face the music on his own.

In Brighton I retraced my steps and booked into the same cheap hotel where Chris and I had once stayed. I had fifty pounds in cash and a gold chain round my neck which might fetch a similar sum. I couldn't keep any food in my stomach as I was going through the withdrawal process from my short but intensive heroin habit. The first two days which I spent mostly in bed were the worst. During this period the familiar whisper of suicide in my head was loud. On the third day I could eat a little and felt like venturing out to a gay pub. Much to my surprise I met an eighteen-year-old blond German student keen to come back to my room. I was surprised for two reasons. He wasn't on the game and he was in Brighton attending a series of forensic lectures as part of his training as a police cadet.

He left me shortly after midnight and lying in the dark unable to sleep the solution to the predicament I was in became startlingly clear. It came into my head as plain as the spoken words. 'The French Foreign Legion.' All I knew about its existence had come from a *Sunday Times* supplement feature which I'd picked up in the lounge of the Manchester YMCA some three months before. I could only remember one sentence which had stayed with me. It read: 'The Paris recruitment centre in France was incongruously situated in the middle of a suburban housing estate'. I'd retained nothing else from the article but I felt the certainty of fate confirming that as my destination.

CHAPTER 16

I LEFT ENGLAND AT THE SAME TIME THAT BRITISH ARMED FORCES were preparing for war with Argentina. I was afraid that my name and description might have been circulated by the police to all ports and air terminals but the customs officer at Dover waved me through with scarcely a glance. Standing on the deck of the ship in the warm evening sunshine I watched the white cliffs receding into the distance and felt quite sure I was travelling towards my death. I assumed I'd be shot either in the desert or in jungle combat. The ferry docked at Calais and I walked with the other passengers out of the terminal without being challenged. There wasn't a train leaving for Paris till the morning so I booked into a small hotel for the night. I was shown to a room with a large iron bed frame and old fading wallpaper. In place of a sink there was a jug filled with water and a hand-painted bowl. I felt a distinct impression of having been there before. The furniture and the history of the room seemed to put me in touch with something familiar yet forgotten. England had become part of a dream and being in France seemed the most natural thing in the world.

I stepped off the train which carried me from Calais to Paris at midday. I had no idea how I would discover the whereabouts of the Legion recruitment office and although the couple of people I'd spoken to had a rudimentary grasp of English I didn't fancy the idea of approaching a complete stranger and asking directions. I had about twenty pounds left which I changed into French francs and asked a taxi driver to take me to the British Embassy. I explained to the clerk behind the desk who spoke with a Scots accent that I was searching for my brother who had left home the day before leaving a note to say he'd gone to join the Foreign Legion. I wanted to know where I could begin looking for him. He was obviously used to enquiries about the Legion and reached down behind the counter and handed me a piece of paper on which the address of Fort Nogerne was neatly typed along with a map showing how to get there on the Metro.

Fort Nogerne stood squat and square at the end of a private driveway. My first thought on catching sight of the place was of Rin Tin Tin and the seventh cavalry. The flag fluttering in the breeze above the stone battlements reminded me of the wooden toy forts of childhood and comic strips. A soldier dressed in olive green combat fatigues stood guarding the main entrance with a machine gun strapped across his chest. He seemed to guess I'd come to join up and without speaking pointed to a waiting room just inside the barrier. There were three other men sitting on the bench inside – they all looked a lot tougher than me. Over the next hour we were joined by four other potential recruits. I was beginning to have second thoughts about waiting much longer when an Indian looking man with three yellow stripes on his sleeve came into the room. From the responses of the others in the room I assumed he was asking in French each one's nationality. He took an immediate interest when I said British and beckoned me to follow him. Walking across what I assumed to be the parade ground he spoke to me in English and asked if I was

166

sure I wanted to join. 'It's for five years,' he said. 'You won't be able to change your mind halfway through.' I said I was sure about what I was doing and followed him inside a three-storey building and up a flight of stone stairs. I asked if the other men we'd left in the waiting room would be joining up. My escort replied that they weren't suitable Legion material. I was puzzled as to how he had reached that conclusion.

The Indian soldier who, from the stripes he wore I guessed was a sergeant, took me into an office and told me to empty my pockets and place the contents on the desk. He asked me questions about my background my family and my employment history, entering the information on a form in front of him. I gave him Chris's name as my own and relied heavily on my knowledge of the family in Devon to fabricate other answers. He asked if I would like to have a new name for my Legion career. I'd already given him one false one, another made little difference. He let me choose and for no good reason I invented the name Simon Rhodes. The last thing he wanted to know was whether I was wanted by the English police for any offences. I assured him I wasn't and followed him out of the office to a room across the passage where a group of men sitting on plastic chairs were gazing idly at an ancient television set. One of them was an English-speaking South African who introduced himself as John. As we shook hands I remembered to say my name was Simon. In conversation I learnt that he had previous military experience with the then Rhodesian army but he was concerned that the shrapnel still lodged in his knee would prevent him passing the Legion's medical and fitness examination. We made a pact that until the worst happened we'd stick together.

When the door opened next it was the Indian sergeant with another recruit. 'Does anyone here speak English?'

167

John waved him over to where we were sitting. He was young, no more than twenty, and his hair was the colour of deep golden red. I would have thought him handsome had it not been for the thick ugly scar which began at the corner of his full lips and gouged a track through the side of his pale-skinned face to the top of his ear. My first reaction was disappointment – if it hadn't been for his disfigurement I would have fancied him. He shook hands with John and I and introduced himself as Luke. I could tell from his voice that his roots were in Glasgow. The other recruits in the room came from all over the world. They were all, without exception, a few years younger than me, the average age being about twenty-three. I hadn't eaten all day and was relieved when the sergeant returned at about six, took us down the stone steps and marched us as a group across the square to a canteen with trestle tables laden with bowls of steaming stew. I was less happy about being picked with three others to stay behind and do the washing up when the meal was over.

The first French world I learnt was *corvette*. Translated into English it meant work of a skivvying kind. Fort Nogerne, as well as being a recruitment centre, was a transit point for Legionnaires either joining or returning from tours of duty with the various regiments scattered around the globe. From bits of information we gleaned it transpired that the group of recruits I was with and whose number was increasing daily would be staying at the fort for a week before being taken by rail to a military camp in the south of France for final selection tests. While we waited our days, which began at five, would be filled with duties in the kitchen or cleaning other areas of the fort. Our civilian clothing had been exchanged for rough brown cast-off army jackets and trousers and our hair cropped close to the scalp. My reflection in the wash room mirror was that of an old style convict. The week at the fort eventually passed and at about eight in the evening John, Luke and I clambered with a score of other recruits into the back of a military lorry. Four compartments of a train had been reserved and the two corporals escorting us said we weren't to leave the carriage to which we'd been allocated other than to use the toilet. We would be travelling all night so we should try and get some sleep.

It was dark outside as the train left Paris and much of the night was spent in trying in predict what we faced at the end of the journey. Luke and I repeatedly reassured John he was sure to pass the medical. We looked forward to the time when our five years in the Legion would be up, talked about how we would keep together during that period and then when it was over how we'd earn fantastic sums of money as freelance mercenaries. Just as the early light of dawn began creeping across the sky Luke climbed into the narrow luggage rack above our heads and fell soundly asleep. I turned my attention to the mountains towering over the train and for the first time in my life felt a sense of awe at the natural beauty of the world and it sunk home to me that I really was in another country.

At the end of our journey we clambered onto the back of another military lorry and drove a mile or so to the premier regiment headquarters of the Legion. The white stone barrack buildings looked immaculate in the seven o'clock sunshine. There was a lot of activity going on: soldiers in green fatigues were unloading lorries, a band was playing as it marched up and down the parade ground in front of a massive bronze memorial. If I wasn't mistaken I could see side shows and stalls similar to those at English style fêtes being erected. Over a welcome cup of black coffee and bread served with a slab of chocolate we learnt our arrival had coincided with the festival of Camarone, the Legion's annual celebration to commemorate their most illustrious battle honours. In its early history a small company of Legionnaires commanded by a pay corps captain had fought heroically against a regiment of Mexican soldiers. Once we had been allocated bunks in the dormitories it was Fort Nogerne routine with a vengeance. John, Luke and myself spent the next four days sweating in the kitchen cleaning out huge vats, peeling thousands of spuds and washing greasy trays clean. Medical examinations, intelligence tests and interviews with the security department were sandwiched between work details. John's fears bore fruit and seven days later he was passed medically unfit and shown the door.

I was secretly pleased John had disappeared from the scene. I'd been growing increasingly irritated by Luke's enquiries as to where he was and what he was doing at all times of the day. The warmth in his tone of voice whenever he mentioned John's name reminded me uncomfortably of Alex back in England in a prison cell, how he used to smile and the little things he did which made me feel I had a friend. Every day another batch of recruits were told they weren't wanted and by the end of three weeks the original group I'd left Fort Nogerne with had been cut down to a quarter. Luke and I passed the final hurdle within minutes of each other. It had become common knowledge that the last test to pass was with the security people. If you walked out of the office without witnessing a red stamp being pressed on your personal file you knew you were out. Luke and I shook hands outside their office: we had made it. My background borrowed from Chris had passed inspection. The past was behind me. My name was Simon, pronounced the French way. I was safe from the robbery squad in London and in a few days Luke and I would be joining a group of thirty other engagee volunteers to start basic training at a camp near the Spanish border.

We had our first taste of real Legion discipline the

170

moment we arrived there. We were greeted by two corporals who screamed at us to unpack the kit we'd been issued. A Legion version of 'O'Grady Says' took place as the corporals held up each item and impatiently waited for us to identify what he was holding and to respond in mirror fashion. Any of the recruits who was a bit slow received a sharp dig in the ribs from one of the corporals who walked amongst them growling in an incomprehensible language. The worst of the two was a black man in his late twenties. On the couple of occasions we exchanged glances I was instinctively aware he came from a culture where respect and deference to an older black man was deeply ingrained. In the hour it took to check our kit I knew I was right. Every other member of the group felt his bunched fist.

After the kit check we were crammed into a barrack dormitory where the top bunk beds almost touched the ceiling. In the narrow space between each sleeping place were five-foot high grey lockers. The rest of the first day and late into the night was spent stowing away our kit by folding it in exact proportions. When this was done we were marched to the main dining hall where a meal of cold potatoes and horse tongue was served with wine. Other recruits from different sections were eating in the crowded hall. It soon became clear that normal dining etiquette was a thing of the past. If you wanted to eat you grabbed one of the bowls on the table to fill your plate even if it meant pushing someone else away from the food. It was a surprise to learn that Luke was teetotal and I willingly accepted his ration of alcohol. It was compensation for the horse tongue which I had no intention of tasting.

My ability to show a fast pair of heels paid dividends over the next four months of training. The one discipline feared by every recruit was the gruelling weekly eight-kilometre run in full combat gear. This had to be completed within a specific time period and there was a lot of kicking and shoving from the two bullying corporals if anyone looked like they were lagging behind. I became the blue eyed boy of the section commander when I broke the section record for completing the distance. He constantly held me up as an example of what a good Legionnaire was made of. In his eyes I could do no wrong. As a result I missed most of the right handers which were flying liberally around.

For the first time in my life I began getting involved in regular fisticuffs. These fights would invariably involve one of the *Beanoms* assigned to me. A *Beanom* was another recruit who could understand the French language. It was his responsibility to interpret whatever order had been given. The trouble was that most orders came with a threat of punishment if it wasn't carried out swiftly enough. This invariably meant the *Beanom* was too concerned with his own avoidance of being kicked and would leave his partner to manage as best he could. Whenever this happened I'd lose my temper and lash out. The section Commander never said anything directly referring to my latest *Beanom*'s black eye or swollen jaw but I knew he was aware of the scraps I kept getting into and I was pretty sure he approved of the reason why.

Luke along with most of the other lads in the section wanted to become a paratrooper when training was over, the elite of the Legion. The sight of a passing soldier wearing the legendary gold wings on his uniform was looked at by raw recruits with reverence and awe. At thirty-one I was past the age for jumping out of low flying aircraft. I'd always been afraid of heights anyway and was set on returning to the Premier regiment as a bandsman. It wasn't necessary to have any musical knowledge: if you were keen enough they would teach you to play an instrument from scratch. Thoughts of becoming a freelance mercenary disappeared with John. I could see a much better future as a professional musician touring the night clubs of France playing long cool sets of sexy jazz. Luke began getting caught up and enthused by the picture I painted of the future. He probably thought being a musician guaranteed the attention of lots of women. One day while we were taking a breather between the assault course session he announced that instead of applying to become a paratrooper he would stick with me and put down to join the band. I knew another reason he'd changed his mind was because of the friendship which had grown between us and neither of us wanted to be separated from the other.

The most difficult aspect of basic training was trying to get to grips with the French language. There were lessons every day but my brain stubbornly refused to either accept, remember or mentally process the foreign sounds that reached my ears. One of the few things I'd regularly been complemented on back in England was how well I spoke. In France without the facility of words at my disposal I was made to feel dumb and stupid. I found it frustrating to be considered a good soldier from the physical perspective but in the brains department a little bit slow. Luke who had no such difficulty was always at hand to whisper in English what was being said but the ease with which he picked up French made me feel pretty stupid as well.

The one other area I failed miserably in was the firing range. I knew how to line the sight up, hold the gun steady and squeeze not pull the trigger. What I found impossible was to prevent myself flinching each time I heard the loud crack of gunfire. The muffles worn like headphones didn't help much and lying down on the range with a dozen other guns firing I jumped involuntarily with every bang. The few times I did manage to hit the target were a result of pure chance.

Eventually the weeks of drill, raid marches and learning other military skills came to an end and Luke with myself and three other lads passed out of the camp wearing the white *képi* on our heads which proclaimed us as fully fledged legionnaires. The train which carried us back to the Legion's premier regiment barracks was crowded and without an escort of corporals and a month's wages in our pockets we were free to make frequent visits to the buffet for cans of beer. I got into a conversation with an attractive American girl who was holidaying in France. She spoke first asking what the uniform I was wearing signified. She was curious to learn more about the Legion and after a few drinks it felt as if we'd known each other for years. Luke and the other lads were impressed by what they saw as my cool pick up. Since joining up I'd kept my sexual orientation deep under cover. The macho image of the Legion wouldn't have tolerated an openly gay soldier. The American girl, whose name was Jennifer, was obviously very attracted to me and because I was quite sloshed I didn't object to the passionate extended kiss she gave me when the train pulled into Aubagne. I promised to write to the address she had given me in the States and walked with the others to the camp, modestly accepting their congratulations on scoring so spectacularly with the girl with the long dark hair.

The music department was housed in a two-storey building set apart from the rest of the barracks complex. A sergeant came out through the plate-glass entrance door and walked down a short flight of concrete steps to meet us. We came to attention as we'd been taught to in training but when I tried to give the expected salute I was so drunk my right hand smacked my white *képi* from my head and onto the ground at my feet. The sergeant's humour wasn't improved by the suppressed giggles from the other lads. He shouted for an orderly who came running and ordered him to take me inside and sober me up with a cold shower. After being assigned bed spaces in a spartan dormitory the sergeant took me into his office. He rattled on for a while giving what I guessed from his tone of voice a rebuke, then reached into a cupboard and handed me a can of beer. There weren't many soldiers in the building and we soon learnt that most of the eighty strong military bandsmen were away on biannual leave leaving only a skeleton staff behind.

I wanted to play saxophone but there was only one left in the stores and this was issued to Luke. I was given a clarinet and told it was the next best thing. Recruits to the band were given a month to decide whether they wanted to stay permanently and feeling disappointed about not getting a saxophone I felt like taking the option of relocation to another regiment. Both Luke and I had misgivings about staying when the rest of the personnel returned from their two-week break. In training, praise and recognition had been earned by performing a given task well but it soon became apparent that the music department functioned on a high level of blatant grovelling. There was an emphasis on drawing attention to someone else's mistake, of attempting to curry favour with the officers at the expense of the man standing next to you. Within days of the band's return we were piling into green coaches and making the long journey by road to Paris. Before setting out, we fresh recruits were given a few perfunctory minutes of marching practice with the rest of the band and then informed we'd be taking part in a parade of massed bands marching down the Champs Elysées as part of Bastille Day celebrations. None of us could play a proper note on the instruments so recently issued to us, but it didn't seem to matter. We were to pretend we were playing like a third of the band already did.

It was a heady experience being dressed in ceremonial

uniform and being applauded and cheered by the thousands lining the route. Shouts of *'Vive le Légion'* rang out from the crowd. I thought for the first time I'd made it into showbiz. Over the next three months we travelled all over France taking part in parades and music festivals. A less pleasant chore was travelling for long distances and standing around for hours waiting for the arrival of the President. It seemed he couldn't alight from a helicopter or car without a sixty-second burst of the national anthem to help him on his way. Back at the base in Aubagne, the day was spent with our instruments practising scales and learning to read music. I already had a rudimentary knowledge of music theory which enabled me to guess most of the time what my French music teacher was getting at in his weekly tutorials.

By November Luke had become disillusioned with life in the Legion and wanted to desert. He wasn't a natural musician and was sick of the bickering and squabbling within the ranks. His social life was also non-existent. The majority of Legionnaires spent most of their free time drinking and although I spent evenings and weekends with him I was invariably drunk while he remained bored and sober. He'd also become confused about our friendship. One evening, even more drunk than usual, I'd blurted out my love for him. He didn't express disgust and admitted he felt distress at not being able to respond to his closest friend's needs. My affection for him had grown steadily over the months we'd been together. When I first met him at Fort Nogerne I'd thought him ugly but almost without my realizing, the scar on his face diminished as a blight and he became more and more beautiful. The security the Legion once seemed to offer Luke was crumbling away. He wasn't sure about anything anymore. He asked me on several occasions to leave with him but I knew that once out of the Legion we would eventually

176

separate – Luke to the love of a woman and me, most likely, to a prison cell.

He left after lunch on a Saturday afternoon. He had a free weekend in front of him which he thought would give him time to get out of the country before the alarm was raised. We'd said our real goodbyes the evening before and he took some photographs with his camera to remember me by.

I watched him walk out of the gate with other soldiers who were going into town for a drink and felt tears stinging my eyes. My sorrow was blunted by an old familiar sense of shock that my brother with the red golden hair was walking out of my life and leaving me. The next day I was representing the Legion in a half marathon race run between Marseilles and the coastal resort of Cassis. I ran hard and fast as if wanting to be punished for losing Luke and on passing the finishing tape I collapsed exhausted on the ground and was rushed to hospital in an ambulance with its siren blaring. The doctor in white hovered above me fixing a saline drip into my arm and listening to my heart with his stethoscope. I couldn't move a muscle. To breathe or even blink seemed an almighty effort. I thought it quite possible I was about to die and I didn't really care.

As a basic grade Legionnaire I was paid the monthly equivalent of one hundred and fifty pounds. Like others, within a few days my wages were squandered on beer drinking sessions round the cafés and bars of Marseilles. My first wage packet had gone on acquiring a civilian wardrobe from the Legion shop which was continually replenished from the backs of newly accepted recruits. I often wondered who had been fortunate enough to buy at a knock-down price the expensive leather jacket I'd worn from England to France. Basic grade soldiers weren't allowed to wear anything but uniform when they left the base. To get round the prohibition I carried my wardrobe past the sergeant on the gate and got changed in the toilet of a nearby café before setting out for a night on the town.

An American Legionnaire I often used to drink with was leaving the band for six months and returning to Castelnaudary to undergo the rigorous sergeant's promotion course. It was against the rules but he had been renting a small bedsit room in Marseilles. He asked if I'd like to take over the tenancy for the monthly rent of three hundred francs. It was almost a quarter of my wages but I jumped at the opportunity. I needed somewhere private. Preoccupied for months with adjusting to a completely new environment, sex had all but drifted out of my consciousness. The prospect of a place of my own however revitalized my interest. My American friend spoke about the girls he had taken to the room. I thought about the boys who might possibly cross the threshold.

On the last pay day before Christmas a bonus was added which more than doubled my usual wages. I decided to be careful how I spent it. I intended to pass the two-day holiday period at my room in Marseilles and it was important I had the financial resources to entertain the recently arrived young Irish recruit who had accepted my invitation to spend Christmas away from the camp. On the night before Christmas Eve I added another two thousand francs to my wallet. I had woken in the night disturbed by the drunken snores of the fully dressed soldier sleeping on the bed next to mine. He was the butt of jokes and derisive comments from other bandsmen. For months he'd been trying to desert and get back to his home in Germany but kept getting caught. He'd spend a month in the cooler then return to the music department before having another attempt at escaping. In the gloom of the dormitory I could make out the shape of his wallet poking out from the pocket of his overcoat. I was confident no one would sympathize if his wages were stolen and most would believe he'd either lost his money or spent it. I slipped out of bed as if going to the bathroom and relieved him of his cash. The following day everybody was busy with the traditional dormitory Christmas crib competition and, as I'd predicted, the man's complaints that he'd been robbed were ignored.

In January the music department all but closed down for the biannual two-week break. Unable to leave France and with no other official residence than the barracks I took advantage of a bed at the Legion's holiday home complex overlooking the Mediterranean. It was somewhere to eat for nothing, a place to buy beer at subsidised prices and at the end of the day a bed in a dormitory shared by half a dozen other men on leave from various regiments. All the money I'd had at Christmas time had been blown on the young Irish soldier who stayed at my bedsit in Marseilles. He was also staying at the holiday home but there was an embarrassed silence between us whenever we met.

Broke and with little else to do other than hang round the Legion bar in the vain hope someone would buy me a beer, I began passing the time by reading a book left behind by my American friend called *Man and his Symbols* by C J Jung. It was the first book in English I'd read in a year. I became completely absorbed by the section which dealt with Jung's theory of the animus. The idea of the female shadow existing in every male resonated deep inside me, releasing from the depths of me vivid images of a gently floating moon. Previous events came back to haunt me. I didn't like myself very much. I cringed at the memory of having spent so much money for the fleeting touch of the young Irish boy's flesh. I felt disgust as I relived slipping stealthily from my dormitory bed to steal my neighbour's Christmas wages. Jung's book held out a vision of the rich potential within the psyche of an individual. I saw myself as shallow and mean in comparison. I might have escaped to the Legion but I was still very much a thief.

By the time I'd finished reading the book I felt impelled to make some kind of gesture. I went looking for the young Irish boy and asked if I could speak to him privately. I'd never been very good at apologizing for anything I'd done but I told him I was very sorry for filling him with drink at Christmas in order to seduce him. He smiled and told me not to worry. He admitted not liking what had happened but was prepared to forget and just be a friend. His generosity made me feel a whole lot better.

It was past ten in the evening and I felt like taking a walk to the nearby beach. I stood on a promontory of giant rocks and looked out across the sea towards a dark smudge of a small island. I'd been told the island had once been a transit point for African slaves being sold into the European market. A storm was brewing and the night sky was unnaturally bright from the light of a huge full yellow moon. Beneath my feet I could hear the breaking waves beginning to grumble. I heard a voice speaking behind me. I turned and saw an old man. He spoke again, warning me a storm was coming and that where I was standing could be dangerous. I gave him a reassuring wave to signal I'd be careful and looked back out to sea. It was then I thought it curious the old man had spoken to me in English. Without really appreciating the transition I was a small child again and I was listening to my father speaking. From a vast distance yet from inside of me I heard him say that 'very soon your life will be completely changed'. I felt a deep fear take hold of me. Apologizing to the Irish boy had had an effect on me and my first thought, and with it fear, was that I would next be saying sorry to the soldier whose wallet I'd stolen. 'Your whole life is going to be completely changed' echoed inside me again and I knew without any doubt I'd caught a glimpse of the future. I called out in my mind, 'I'm frightened.' Then like he did in the night before I was old enough to speak he wrapped me in his love and held me.

Two nights later I was woken from sleep by the drunken noisy return of two soldiers to the dormitory. As if standing outside myself I watched as I climbed out of the bed and got dressed in my legion tracksuit. I had a raging thirst which could only be quenched with alcohol. The most important thing in the world was to get my hands on a drink. A stone's throw from the holiday home was a small bar frequented by Legionnaires. It was three in the morning and by then the lock up premises should have been empty. I walked out of the holiday complex grounds with a nine-inch combat knife strapped to my leg. It would come in useful to force open the cash boxes of the juke box and two fruit machines. A narrow side window protected by iron bars was my safest point of entry and although I knew I was physically fit I was still surprised at being able to pull the bars apart with just my bare hands. Inside the bar I poured myself a stiff drink from the first whisky bottle I found in the dark and then set about locating the cash boxes of the machines. I was out of luck; they were open and had been emptied. Outside I heard a car pulling up which prompted me to make a move away from the scene of the crime. I slipped the two bolts fastening the rear door and was met by two men with pistols aimed directly at my head.

CHAPTER 17

I HAD EXPECTED MY LIFE TO BE CHANGED BUT I DIDN'T EXPECT to be arrested and locked in a police cell similar to so many I'd inhabited in the past. It was late evening and dark by the time the prison bus delivered a group of us from the Palais de Justice to Beaumetz Jail and midnight before reception procedures were over. I was allocated a cell on the highest landing of the cavernous building where I lay exhausted on the hard mattress thinking over what had taken place that day.

The arresting police officers had been in touch with the regiment's commanding officer and had attempted to discover my original name before joining the legion. True to tradition the colonel had told them nothing. Like their British counterparts they tried to get me to admit to other offences. My lack of skill with the French language inhibited their interrogation techniques and they soon tired of my halting answers and handed me on to an examining magistrate. An interpreter was called and it was explained I'd be held in custody pending trial at a later date.

I spent much of that first night back in a prison turning over in my mind what the likely reaction would be when news of my arrest filtered back to the music department. I guessed some would be pleased with my fall from grace, others would see me as a little crazy perhaps but a *'Bon Légionnaire'*. I knew that the Legion hierarchy wouldn't be too fazed by my arrest. It was a Legion tradition that any man returning to camp after serving a prison sentence was automatically given five days paid vacation. Even so I still felt ashamed, as if I'd let the legion down. I felt grateful to the camp commandant for giving the police short shrift but I was still worried that computers or Interpol might identify me and set the process of extradition back to England in motion.

I must have fallen asleep eventually because when I woke the sun was shining into the cell from high in the sky. I lay for a moment confused by my surroundings then it all came back in a rush with the knowledge I'd well and truly messed up. Staring at the paint-chipped ceiling I puzzled over the absence of breakfast. Had I been forgotten? Slept through some kind of call? Or could it be the custom in French jails to feed it's inmates only once a day? It gradually dawned on me how noisy it was. Filtering through the closed window I could hear the sound of raised voices, shouting, laughing and jeers. I thought my cell must overlook the exercise yard, but in English prisons all you would hear was the tread of feet walking in circles and muted conversation. I was eventually forced from the bed by a need to use the pot in the corner of the cell. Glancing out through the barred window the source of the noise became apparent. Near to what looked like the front gate of the prison stood a forty-foot high building; its flat roof was crammed with more than a hundred men, many of whose faces were obscured and muffled by scarves and other pieces of material. Some kind of demonstration was obviously taking place. At the base of the building stood a contingent of riot police carrying guns and holding plastic shields. A civilian dressed in a camel-hair coat stood slightly apart and with the cell window open, I could hear he was addressing the roof-top protestors through a megaphone. The men on the roof began hurling down angry abuse at which camel coat turned to his troops who cocked rifles to their shoulders and began firing CS canisters into the crowd above them. There was a rush to escape from their exposed position but the one route of escape was a solitary flimsy-looking drainpipe. Many of the protestors fell or jumped onto a secondary roof some twenty feet below. Some landed awkwardly and lay in obvious pain from damaged limbs while others tottered perilously close to the edge of the building trying to claw the gas from their eyes.

Towards evening my cell was unlocked and a plate of tasteless food handed in. A little later a trolley came with some books on board. There was only one written in English. It was the true story of a man sailing single-handed round the world. I wouldn't have given it a glance at any other time but over the next couple of days I read it several times. The book helped me escape from the frightening experience of being on my own, the sadness I felt during the half hour exercise period of not being able to communicate with anyone. Almost every inmate I saw was of Arab appearance. One foxy sly-faced individual tried to sell me a carton of cigarettes in exchange for the watch on my wrist but as much as I wanted a smoke I wouldn't part with my only connection with time. I didn't know when my next court appearance was due, nor any idea what would happen there. Worst of all I dreaded the prospect of long lonely hours in a prison cell.

The Chief prison officer came to my rescue. I was unlocked one morning and escorted down to his office. He spoke quite passable English and asked if I would like a job working as an orderly in the hospital. There was already one British Legionnaire working there and he would show me the ropes. I hadn't felt so grateful to anyone in years and responded with an emphatic *Oui* when he asked if the job would suit me. He gave instructions to my escort to take me to the hospital but before doing so there were two Legion officers waiting to see me in an adjoining office. I thought they might have come to say the Legion no longer wanted me but the two sergeants cheered me by saying they had come to check I was being treated alright and to leave me a few cartons of cigarettes. They told me not to worry about money as arrangements had been made for half my monthly wages to be placed in my personal prison account.

The hospital was a two-landing annexe at the edge of the main prison. The ground floor housed the medical pharmacy store, examination rooms and administrative offices, the upper landing was filled down either side with cells. The sign on the heavy oak door separating the hospital from the rest of the prison read *Mutations* in large white lettering. Inside I recognized the familiar atmosphere of places where the sick were cared for. I was met at the door by a smiling prison officer wearing a white coat over his blue uniform shirt and trousers. He took me to a corner cell on the upper landing and introduced me to the English Legionnaire called Roy. He was sitting on the bottom bunk bed swigging from a can of lager. He was a short, thick-looking, pug-faced youth in his early twenties. I took an instant dislike to him but gave a false smile as we were introduced.

Through lips as narrow as the gap in a pencil sharpener Roy outlined the duties of an orderly. 'We give 'em a loaf of bread and a jug of coffee in the mornings,' he said referring to the inmates, 'Serve up dinner and tea, give out and collect the cutlery they use and, once a week, clean laundry.'

'That sounds easy enough,' I remarked. Which led him on to setting out the perks of the job.

'They're all nutters here. Most of them don't know what day it is so when we take their canteen orders there's always an earner to be made.'

I didn't like his tone of voice so to change the subject I asked what he was in for.

'There's three of us altogether. The other two are working in the bath house. We're up for attempted murder.' He went on to explain how he and his two mates had discovered another Legionnaire was queer and they had taken it upon themselves to do him in. Luring him into Marseilles on the pretext of a night on the town they had left him for dead in an alley with his throat slashed and a note pinned to his chest in the form of a death warrant.

Roy was wrong about the forty or so blokes on the wing all being nutters. A few were heavily sedated but only one or two seemed hopelessly deranged. One man was in the hospital for security reasons. He was a prominent member of *Action Direct* the terrorist organization. The others were in the hospital for psychiatric assessment at the court's behest. Serving food through the hatch in the cell doors I soon got to know the residents. Every time I closed the hatch and slid the locking bold I felt a twinge of guilt as well as the growing seeds of compassion. In no time at all I began to see the men as my personal responsibility. It seemed too that some were aware I cared. Much of my considerable spare time was spent with my head poking through the hatch of individual doors trying to hold conversations with my limited command of French. One particular old man was a favourite of mine to spend time with. He had killed his wife and as a result a major part of his mind had shut down in protest. Each morning when I passed him coffee and fresh bread through the hatch I'd find him standing neatly dressed in his pinstripe suit, his silver hair immaculately brushed and shining and a hopeful smile on his face that this was the day he'd be rejoining his wife at home.

A month after starting work as an orderly I was taken out for the day to the Palais de Justice and sentenced to three months imprisonment. With time already served on remand I had about four weeks left to serve.

I considered the sentence lenient by English standards. I wouldn't have minded it being longer – I was quite content working in the prison hospital. I felt a sense of real fulfilment taking care of the inmates' basic needs.

I found another book in the library written in English. It was Thomas à Kempis's *Imitation of Christ*. During the late evening after Roy and I had been locked in the cell I read it slowly while drinking lager from the cans I was able to order from the prison canteen. There was little scope for conversation with my cell mate. An unspoken truce existed between us. I had continually offended him by pointing out how spitefully he viewed and treated the hospital inmates. He couldn't understand either the anger I expressed or my refusal to allow him to substitute the dead batteries from his radio for a set of new ones a patient had ordered from the canteen. In the course of that particular row I shut him up by telling him what a hypocrite he was. He wasn't aware until I told him that I'd seen him passing sweet little love notes to a very effeminate inmate located on the main wing. His face turned pale when I suggested his two Legionnaire friends might be interested considering the background to the offence he'd been charged with.

I spent at least a couple of hours a day in conversation with the terrorist from *Action Direct*. At first I'd been quite resentful of the attention he received. Prison officers from the main prison wing were always finding an excuse to call in at the hospital in order to pop up to his cell for a chat through the hatch of his cell door. He was a kind of celebrity with his picture and name splashed across national newspapers. John was a short stocky man in his early thirties. He wore his hair in a scruffy unruly mop which complimented his Mexican cowboy-style drooping moustache. Before his arrest he'd been employed as a school teacher. The pictures which covered the walls of his cell testified he was also a highly talented artist. At first I wanted to tell him to stop demeaning himself as I watched his face light up whenever a screw came to call. I recognized the gestures of a prisoner anxious to be an attentive host. These men are your jailers, I wanted to say. The way you react to them it looks like you are grovelling. I could see a part of my prison experience in John and part of my resentment came from the jealousy of the attention he received. As the days passed a friendship began to develop between us. He had an engaging personality which linked to his ability with the English language meant we were soon having long discussions about subjects concerning us most.

John had been in prison for only a few months and behind the mask of celebrity status he had adopted was a fear of how he would cope with being locked up for years. He had a wife and young family outside and was concerned about how their feelings might gradually cool towards him. John had been a member of a terrorist cell which had murdered a policeman along with several of his family. One of the victims had been a child just a few months old. During the time he'd been in prison he was moving towards the realization that political causes, however noble, couldn't excuse the murder of a baby.

I'd known what it was like to be racked and tortured with guilt. My reading of *Imitation of Christ* influenced how I discussed the notion of forgiveness with John. Encouraged by John's candidness I told him about my life before the Legion. He wanted to know what plans I'd made for my imminent release. I said I'd be returning to the regimental band but with some reluctance. I still felt a sense of humiliation at being caught in the act of such a dumb crime. I wasn't looking forward to those who would look in my direction and then whisper amongst themselves: 'You see Rhodes over there – well, he screwed up his chances of becoming one of the rare Legionnaires to be promoted through the ranks to commissioned officer status. He had everything going for him. Just before Christmas he won the regimental cross-country race which every soldier in the barracks was obliged by tradition to take part in. While the band played and a thousand men stood to attention the colonel in chief hung a shining silver medal round his neck. Then he went and blew it all a few weeks later by getting sent to prison.'

I spoke to John about an alternative option I'd been toying with: returning to England as a penitent sinner, throwing myself at the mercy of the court and hoping the judge would take account of the sincere wish I had of making a new life for myself. John's response was to say that if I chose such a course of action I would one day become a household name. He made the remark quite spontaneously and as soon as the words were out I wanted to believe him.

The experience of working in the prison hospital was having a deep effect on me. I'd lived amongst prisoners for years but caring for those who were sick brought home to me how precious each one of them was. I felt for them most intensely when the tranquillity of my life was shattered by an overwhelming mixture of anger and compassion each time a suicide attempt was made. These acts usually occurred late and would be discovered by the passing night patrol. I would be woken, summoned from my cell and the scene to greet me was invariably the same: dark red arterial blood staining the bleached white uniform of attending medics, thick red blood soaking through the blankets and sheets on the prison bed and a grey almost lifeless body lying helpless in the mess of his own creation. The intensity of the anger I felt always shocked me. It was as if I, too, had experienced the terrible desperation which pushed a man as far as destroying his own life. To feel such pain and distress seemed truly wicked. Back in my cell I'd find sleep impossible – my mind would be filled with images of blood and suffering, of scooping up blood from the floor too thick to disperse with a mop, of having to use a shovel instead to scrape the blood into a black plastic dustbin. At times I imagined I felt as Jesus must have felt. Deeply moved by the plight of the sick and demanding nothing in return for his care, yet thrilled if the warmth of his love was recognized.

In the few days before I was due to leave the prison I felt a close affinity with the Jesus of the Gospels. Like a child playing his own private game I invited him into the cell for tea and biscuits. I pictured him sitting with me at the small wooden table. I fussed around him concerned that the cushion he sat on was soft enough. There were no sermons or clever parables. Just me taking care of a valued friend.

On my final night in the prison hospital I lay in the darkened cell with the sound of Roy breathing heavily asleep as a background to my thoughts. When morning came I'd visit every cell handing out bread and black coffee for the very last time. There would be tears not far away as I said goodbye to the friends who had come to mean so much to me. They had shown me how it felt to be needed and the experience had brought me to life. Unable to sleep I knew I had a decision to make which would change the course of my life. I was afraid that I might be fooling myself, like the time more than a year previously when I'd returned to Manchester to hand myself in to the police. At about midnight I gave up the furious debate ringing in my head by passing the buck and saying, 'Jesus, if I manage to get back to England without being captured as a deserter, then I'll know for sure I'm doing your will.' With the decision made I fell peacefully asleep.

It was still dark in the cell when I was woken by the presence of a ghost. Not the malevolent menacing image conjured up in the frightened imagination of a child but a red golden flame burning warmly inside me. In that moment I knew the answer to everything I'd ever wanted to know. My father was real and whatever the future held my life was to be completely changed.

postscript

MORE THAN TEN YEARS HAVE PASSED SINCE I WALKED OUT OF the Legion camp to climb aboard a train and head for the relative safety of Belgium. I admitted to the Belgian customs officers that I was deserting the Legion and making for the British Embassy in Brussels. They responded by saying they hadn't seen me and wished me luck! In Brussels, a surprised Embassy official, whom I told that I was wanted by Chelsea robbery squad, arranged for a car to get me to Ostend and for the police to meet me when the midnight ferry reached Dover. Four months later, I was sentenced to twelve years' imprisonment. Although I'd expected a long sentence, I was still a bit numb when I reached Wandsworth's long-termers' wing. Alex, my robbery partner, was by coincidence in the same prison, a year into his ten-year sentence. It was good to be reunited, especially when I learned that he, too, had spent a few months in the Foreign Legion. As luck would have it, we were both transferred to the Isle of Wight shortly afterwards.

I was determined not to waste the years I spent locked up. I started to record my experiences in a journal, with the idea I might have enough material for a book by the time I was released, and I put my name down for an Open

University degree course. I was even prepared to be separated from Alex when, eighteen months into my sentence, I was offered a transfer to Lewes prison where educational facilities were better than those available on the island. Lewes prison was just a few miles from where I went to school on the South Coast: I had come full circle.

My first tutor for the O.U. Arts Foundation Course was an earth mother-type called Lindy Jordan who, over the years, became my best friend. She was my main source of support both emotionally and materially, and her weekly tutorials became, in effect, social visits. During my second year of study, I made instant friends with Christine Grey, who came into the prison to tutor me in psychology. After the first tutorial, she instinctively kissed me goodbye on the cheek only to be told by a member of the prison staff that such displays of affection could lead into potentially compromising situations! Although the course lasted only eight months, Christine continued to visit me for the remainder of my sentence and, to give added weight to my annual parole applications, she offered me a room in her Brighton home when I was eventually released.

Studying at university level was an illuminating experience. As my powers of analysis developed, I gained the confidence to be more creative in my daily journal, *Wings and Landings*. In 1987 I showed it to the prison's writer in residence who was impressed enough to suggest my work was even publishable. From then on I began submitting articles to magazines and journals but my future as a writer only became a realistic possibility when Chris Paling, a Radio 4 Producer, was allowed into the prison to record the working life of Stephen Plaice, the resident writer. Steve asked me to get involved, and I suggested that, rather than sitting in the slightly sterile environment of the Education Complex, Chris came onto the wing and used my cell as his headquarters. It worked well, and for two weeks I got some first-hand experience of how a radio programme was made. As soon as *Whispers on the Wing* was broadcast, I knew I'd been involved in something approaching excellence and I wanted more!

The next opportunity came on 9 September 1990. My last parole application had been successful and, after seven and a half years in jail, I was met outside the gate by Chris who wanted to record my thoughts and feelings about being free. It was a very emotional period for me but I had complete trust in Chris, who invited me into his home with his wife Julie, daughter Sarah and, a few months later, his son Thomas. I'm still a frequent visitor to their house and the pub round the corner where Chris and I sink a few pints. *On the Out* was well received by the critics and Chris suggested we make a series of six fifteen-minute programmes based on my *Wings and Landings* journal. It was to be our most successful yet, with rave reviews in the national press. I was even invited on to Radio 4's prestigious *Start the Week* with Melvyn Bragg.

Chris didn't stop with that series; before coming out of prison I'd shown him the first draft of *Silver Threads* which he suggested I take to BBC Books. Heather Holden-Brown, Senior Commissioning Editor, agreed to publish it and Michael Green, the Controller of Radio 4, commissioned a series of recorded extracts. At the time of writing, *Silver Threads* is at page-proof stage after being constructively edited by Doug Young and I've promised yet again to get this postscript off to him for late inclusion.

Not content with simply writing, which I find an isolating experience, I've dipped my toe into the world of theatre. Stephen Plaice still works at Lewes prison, and we meet frequently in Brighton. In 1993 we completed a satirical two-man show called *Whose Crime is it Anyway?* in which we take to the stage to perform a series of vignettes which received enthusiastic applause at both

Brighton and Edinburgh Festivals. I like being on the stage. I enjoy playing to a live audience and especially making them laugh. There's a possibility of the show being taken to America though my past may prove to be an obstacle to getting a visa.

During my two-week trip to Edinburgh, a city I fell in love with, the most frequent question was, 'What are you going to do next?' Whatever I choose, I feel sure that it shouldn't be based on my particular past, that I should take on the challenge of returning to the stage in a role other than ex-felon just to find out whether anybody would still come and see me.

A few days ago I celebrated the third anniversary of my release from Lewes prison – I'm still not sure how well I've adjusted to the outside world. I'm disappointed with my inability to establish the loving partnership with the guy I was sure would be waiting for me out here. But it's not too late and, although sometimes I feel lonely, life outside prison is certainly preferable. And, while I wait, I have a wide circle of friends and the ready-made but noisy family of Jelly – my Heinz 57 dog – and the recent addition of a bossy little Yorkshire terrier.